Praise for *Coming Into Your Own*

"Solid in theory, sound in perspective, and carried on the wings of real stories, Barbara Cecil offers a trustworthy guide to the cycles of a woman's life. Cecil's writing is wholly/holy common sense, integrating years of listening and gentle leading. Follow this voice, walk this labyrinth of learning, and join the company offered you here on the necessary journey of becoming and being your fullest self."

–Christina Baldwin, author of *Life's Companion, Journal Writing as Spiritual Practice,* and *Storycatcher, Making Sense of Our Lives through the Power and Practice of Story*

"As countless people around the world join hands and hearts in service to a life-sustaining future, they discover that the personal is political. This is especially true for women as they hearken to the calls for change in their own lives. For this transformative journey, Barbara Cecil provides a trustworthy map for coming into our own."

–Joanna Macy, author, *Coming Back to Life*

"The future of leadership will be more feminine, conscious, and collective. *Coming Into Your Own* offers intriguing real-life examples and core practices for this new, inner leadership work. Highly recommended!"

–Otto Scharmer, co-founder of The Presencing Institute, author, *Theory U,* co-author, *Leading from the Emerging Future*

"Barbara is a master at creating hospitable spaces in which we, as women, can remember our deeper callings and stand in our full stature. The crises and turning points we face personally and professionally demand a wholesome context and the kind of 'time and space apart' that Barbara and her colleagues create so beautifully. With great sensitivity she has done the very same thing in a special book that supports women across cultures as they consciously navigate their life transitions. *Coming Into Your Own* is a gift to all of us."

–Juanita Brown, PhD., co-founder, The World Cafe and co-author, *StoryBridge: From Alienation to Community Acti*

D1475394

"*Coming Into Your Own* is a wonderful guide for living our best lives. In a personal and intimate way, Barbara uses the stories of remarkable women to give us a tangible feel for how change can happen in a way that leads to a solid sense of self and fulfillment. This book is a must read for anyone who confronts change and adversity in her life. That means it is a must read for all of us! I can already think of hundreds of people I want to give it to."

–Robin Miller, MD, Medical Director, Triune Integrative Medicine Clinic/ Medical Reporter, KOBI-NBC/Member of the Executive Advisory Board of Sharecare

"In the 'untidy mess of personal transition,' it can be difficult to find your way; this book provides much-needed light for the journey. *Coming Into Your Own*, much like the author's seminars of the same name, provides wise and gentle guidance for navigating life's transitions and nudges the reader towards self-confidence and self-trust, joy, and fulfillment of her own unique soul-purpose. What Lauren Artress did for the ancient spiritual tool of the labyrinth in her book *Walking a Sacred Path*, Barbara Cecil does for women's circles and a deeply felt, feminine approach to the cycles of life."

–M.C. Sungaila, law firm partner, bar and community leader, nonprofit board member, author, and CIYO alumna

"Give yourself the gift of time to sink into the soul-deep wisdom of this book. If you are in the turmoil of transition, elder woman and wise guide Barbara Cecil will help you to find purpose, peace, and a pathway through the chaos that is right for you."

–Sarah Rozenthuler, consultant, psychologist, and author of *Life-Changing Conversations*

"The understanding of how profound change works described in this book was born out of experimentation, courage, and astute reflection in a mature, long-standing women's circle. It is thrilling to me that our pioneering is now available to support and inspire women and women's circles far and wide. The beauty of the book is congruent with the character of the author."

–Anne Dosher, PhD, social services consultant and activist, elder

"Whoever you are, wherever you are on your life journey, this book will hit home. It speaks to me personally, and will be a treasured companion to the women I travel with in these remarkable times."

–Dee Anne Everson, executive director, United Way of Jackson County, Oregon

"Casting back over the years, I remember specific times when my current story, once so savory in my mouth, went stale and dry, when I felt confused and bereft, unable to go backwards or forwards, trying a few things but nothing sticking. Then, as if in my peripheral vision, a speck of inspiration came, so small it slipped past any grandiosity and something new, unexpected was born. I wish I had had Barbara Cecil's map of change, then, to surround the shakiness I felt and remind me of life's trustworthiness. Here in this book you now have access to her gentle wisdom, born of her willingness to go deep down in herself and with others, to find the pearls of truth."

–Vicki Robin, co-author, *Your Money or Your Life;* author, *Blessing the Hands That Feed Us*

Coming Into Your Own

A Woman's Guide
Through Life Transitions

Barbara Cecil

Afterword by Margaret J. Wheatley

Barbara Cecil

White Cloud Press
Ashland, Oregon

White Cloud Press books may be purchased for educational, business, or sales promotional use. For information, please write:

Special Market Department, White Cloud Press, PO Box 3400, Ashland, OR 97520

Website: www.whitecloudpress.com

Cover and Interior Design by C Book Services

Printed in the United States

First edition: 2015
15 16 17 18 19 20   10 9 8 7 6 5 4 3 2 1

Library of Congress Cataloging-in-Publication Data

Cecil, Barbara.
 Coming into your own : a woman's guide through life transitions / by Barbara Cecil. -- First edition.
    pages cm
 ISBN 978-1-935952-60-2 (paperback)
1. Life change events. 2. Career changes. 3. Self-realization in women. 4. Women--Psychology. I. Title.
 BF637.L53C43 2015
 158.1--dc23
                                        2015013019

Dedication

I dedicate this book to the women all over the globe who are stepping into their full stature and present-day callings. You lead the way for women everywhere whose lives are in transition, and who are determined to find, in the midst of turmoil, their unique pathway into the future. Your strength, beauty, and courage are shining inspirations. The well-being of our world cries out for the power, beauty, and wisdom of women who are coming into their own.

Contents

Prologue

My mother is in a nursing home, 2,800 long, costly miles from my home in Ashland, Oregon. I travel to North Carolina to be with her as often as I can, and we talk by phone at least once every day. Despite the distance and her dementia, there is an intimacy between us that I never knew in earlier years.

My mom, Phyllis Magat, was the first woman to earn a Ph.D. in chemistry from MIT. Armed with her degree, she went to work at the DuPont Company, eager to contribute to leading-edge research. However, the men to whom she reported, imagining there was something more fitting for a woman, insisted she work in the company library. The head librarian, most likely jealous of my mother's educational status, sought to put her in her place with near-impossible research translation in four languages. After three trying years, feeling humiliated, and having worked far beyond her designated hours to complete her assignments, my mother finally resigned.

She then taught chemistry at Swarthmore College, a respected liberal-arts institution in Pennsylvania with a reputation for excellence in the sciences. From there, she went on to focus on developing a math and science curriculum for a large school district, and later became a superintendent. In my memories of childhood, she was rarely at home: always at work or, in the evenings, at a professional meeting—except, once a year, for happy vacations when we went camping as a family.

When I was one year old, Chanie, our housekeeper, had stepped in to care for my brother and me, and she stayed with us through our graduation from high school. During those years of my childhood, my mother seemed to serve mostly as a disciplinarian. So it was Chanie, not my mom, in whom I confided at crucial growing-up moments—such as when I first got my period, at age 12. She reassured me that I wouldn't bleed to death, then strapped me into the harness contraption that held the pad in place.

Decades later, however, I have come to appreciate the gifts my mother gave me during her years of relative absence from my life. Following graduate school, I became a management consultant. Twenty years into that line of work, I began to specialize in supporting women leaders.

It was only then that I understood what a light my mother had been to women and girls as she persisted in her education and her science career in what was then a man's world. At age 91, she was given an award for excellence for her work as a teacher sixty years earlier, inspiring high school girls who would hardly have imagined a career in math or science until they met a woman who had earned a Ph.D. in chemistry.

Like my mother, I have dedicated my life to helping women in many parts of the world find their voice, their confidence, and their calling. Twenty years ago, with Glennifer Gillespie and Beth Jandernoa, I co-founded Coming Into Your Own (CIYO), a program that helps women around the world navigate their way through the upheaval and excitement of life transitions. To this day, before every CIYO retreat, I make a point of calling my mother, who, despite her failing memory, soundly blesses me and the women in these groups. We both know that I am continuing her work as a champion for women who long to fulfill their potential and follow their dreams.

On the afternoon of Thanksgiving Day in 2013, missing my mother, I telephoned her. I pictured her in her usual position in her recliner, feet up, watching TV. She answered with her predictable opener: "Barbara, so good to hear your voice. What do I need to know?" She usually asked that question as a way of avoiding having to speak about herself in a coherent way. A staunch New Englander with Lutheran-Swedish roots, she rarely expressed her feelings or reflected openly on her life. But that day, the fog in her mind lifted for a short while, and we had a special conversation that became a treasure for me.

I answered with my usual, "Mom, I walked the dog, and I've been working on my book."

As usual, she asked, "What's the book about and who is it for?" But this time, when I explained that it was about women handling transitions in their lives, she said, "I have something to say about what transition meant to me in my life."

I quickly grabbed pen and paper. She proceeded to tell me that it was during her periods of transition that she had had "revelations." I had never heard her use that word before. Talking about transitions between job assignments, she said, "At those times of change, I felt a 'yearning.'"

This was another word I'd never heard her use. What was the yearning about?

She said, "I felt envy"—yet another word I hadn't known was in her lexicon—"toward others who had time to garden and talk with women friends about the things that mattered to them."

How had she worked with these feelings?

"I had no time to socialize or participate in women's discussion groups," she went on, "but once I did manage to fit in a women's investment group. We pooled our money, talked about market trends, then invested our collective kitty." The memory made her laugh. "We made good money. I bought my cherrywood desk with the earnings."

She then explained why she had hired Chanie. "I planned menus and bought food, but I asked Chanie to cook dinners so that, in the little time I had after work and before evening meetings, I could work outdoors. I remember a large pile of dirt outside my bedroom window that I'd sink my hands into for relief when I finally got home late in the afternoon. Whenever I was touching the earth, my tension and worries disappeared, along with my envy of other women."

She took in a sharp breath. "I am having a memory—one that I had forgotten until this very moment. I'm remembering the apple tree outside my bedroom window. That apple tree and I had a relationship. We spoke to each other every day. I've never told this to anyone, including your father, because they would have thought I was crazy. I would help the apple tree bloom by reminding her when it was time. We figured out the timing together. She needed me, and I needed her. We blossomed together. There were other apple trees in the yard that I thanked regularly for what they gave. But this one tree spoke back to me and was a great source of happiness. That happiness spread into all other parts of my life."

My turn for a sharp in-breath. Was this the same left-brained chemist who taught me how to make muffins while explaining the differing chemical reactions of baking soda and baking powder? *I hardly know this woman*, I thought. That conversation would play a part in undoing many images and judgments of my mother that I'd held for years.

Tears rose in me as I glimpsed the trajectory of my own life, seeded so long ago in my mother's story. I saw decades of my work coaching and guiding women as they grew into their full stature and callings—my own version of my mother's dedication to breaking the glass ceiling.

And I saw my own yearnings to both follow a growing intimacy with the natural world and fulfill my longing to engage in the potential of the compelling connection women can have with one another.

Some of the core messages of this book were contained in my mother's ruminations during that phone conversation. Just as her life was shaped by a call to work in the sciences at a time when the dominant culture discouraged women from entering the field, many of the women I have worked with are likewise urged by an inner call to tread a unique path for which they are innately suited. I have come to understand this merger of one's own predispositions with the world's needs at a particular time as the "soul's journey." I have written this book to help you clarify what that means for your own life.

That Thanksgiving Day conversation with my mom revealed to me, for the first time, the rich quality of my mother's character that had been the carrier wave for all she had outwardly accomplished. Her stories about finding respite in the dirt pile, her ability to communicate with "her" apple tree, even her longing for richer friendships with women, all reflect an understanding of a universal web of life. She engaged with those breaks in her busy life to fulfill her yearning to participate in this miraculous web.

The ache I felt at my mother's absence during my growing-up years has now been filled by gratitude for all she has given me, and by the tenderness we have come to share. Our Thanksgiving Day conversation closed with this exchange:

"Mom, thank you so much for trusting me with these personal stories. This upcoming move Michael and I are making will start with a search for an apple orchard."

"Remember, Barbara," she said before hanging up, "you don't need an orchard. You only need one tree."

I now understand what my mother was telling me: "Remember who you are." When I speak in this book about knowledge of "Self" or "becoming more conscious," I am saying the same thing to you: "Remember who you are." It is my hope that *Coming Into Your Own: A Woman's Guide Through Life Transitions* will give you the means to connect with your deeper Self, and to the sacred, life-giving force that informs all of creation. May you open to the reliability and potency of this force as it seeks to re-align your life's current shape with a form of your calling that is relevant for this stage of your life and the world as it is today. It is my conviction that what is happening for you at this time is the perfect ground for your next steps on your journey to wholeness.

Barbara Cecil

Ashland, Oregon

In these pages you will find forthright and true stories of women who have explored deeply what it means to come into their own amid the pressures and seductions of the world around them. Since our approach in the Coming Into Your Own courses includes the facilitators being transparent about their own learning experiences, I include some of my stories here as well. These periods of change in our lives are rich in wisdom because, as my mother reminded me, they are the times when we are most sensitive to a soul-deep call that beckons us into the deeper stream of our life purpose.

The friends, colleagues, and graduates of CIYO whom you will meet in the pages that follow come from Asia, Africa, Europe, the Near East, and North America. For the most part, their stories are told here using their real names. I have respected their own wording, and appreciate their candor in service to others who are passing through transitions. The body of experience and wisdom that CIYO has amassed over the decades lives in these pages.

1

The Wheel of Change: The Four Phases of Transition

*I*s life asking you to let go of habits, beliefs, people, or images of yourself? Have major themes in your life come to a conclusion, leaving you in a void, unsure of what's next? Do you feel at a loss, with no energized direction in sight? Are you in need of healing, or time out to reflect? Are new options percolating? Or are you primarily stewarding a long-term focus that requires tenacity and dedication?

Your answers to these questions will be clues to the stage of the life transition process you are currently in. The ensuing chapters will help you identify this stage, and understand what is needed here to connect to your deeper calling and the core sense of Self that beckons through the chaos of change.

When we are steeped in the untidy mess of personal transition, it often seems as if there is no order at all in the upheaval. In fact, the opposite is true, although it is difficult to see when you are in the midst of change. But if you consciously engage the journey rather than resist it, within the turmoil you will find a trajectory that will carry you through to a new phase of your life, one more closely aligned with your soul's calling. As you will see in the following story, there are four reliable stages of transition. These will be further explained through the Wheel of Change, so that you can begin to understand the process, and successfully navigate whichever phase has arisen in your own journey.

One of the greatest joys in my life is witnessing a woman standing in her full stature, thoroughly herself, at ease in the world. Maaianne (*May-YAN*) carried this quality of presence. I had watched her, each year for almost a decade, stand up in front of hundreds, sometimes thousands, of people from around the world. In her thirties, she was already the founder of a management-consulting company in South Africa. On those annual occasions when our paths intersected, Maaianne was in her role as emcee of a conference on "authentic leadership." She was known as the "weaver" who brought together the threads of plenary sessions, workshops, logistics, and spontaneous inspirations from a team of talented artists. Behind the microphone she was unassuming but polished, bathing the audience in the warmth of her broad smile.

One year I watched, deeply moved, as Maaianne's radiant demeanor dissolved. I was hosting an impromptu circle at the event—about 25 men and women sharing the questions we were privately asking ourselves about our personal life journeys. One of the participants was Michael Jones, a pianist and a dear friend. He proceeded to share his self-inquiry in the language of improvised music. His playing alternated between swells of confidence and dips into tentative self-questioning. Others, ranging from professionals to aspiring leaders, revealed their secret doubts and hopes in words.

Then came Maaianne's turn to speak. At a loss for words, she quietly wept. In the language of the heart, she "spoke" of the unnamable sorrow and confusion that were growing in her, telling the story of a life that was falling apart.

After the gathering, I sought her out. "I have been collecting poems on the theme of transitions, and I'd be glad to send them to you." Maaianne gratefully accepted. Thus began an exchange of stories and poetry that spanned four years and the distance between South Africa and the United States. Over this time I had the privilege of walking with Maaianne through her slide into despair, followed by a great void and then, gradually, her profound reinvention of herself.

Maaianne had it all at an early age: a loving husband, two beautiful children, a nice house, two dogs, two cars, and a successful business that was making a significant contribution to the complex issues facing South Africa.

For as long as she could remember, Maaianne had always known what to do and what direction to follow . . . until she lost her way. For no apparent reason, she began to lose her sense of purpose. That familiar drive drained out of her. "My life went onto autopilot. . . . I was doing whatever I was doing because I felt I had to." Instead of enjoying her work as before, Maaianne began to see that she was running her company out of a sense of responsibility to her partners, not wanting to let them down. Besides, it was income that covered her family's mortgage payment.

"The idea that the life I'd been living was 'as good as it gets' filled me with quiet terror. My joyful soul was hidden in some out-of-the-way recess of my life." Maaianne descended into depression, believing that the brightest and most meaningful moments of her life were behind her, yet ashamed to admit this to her family and friends for fear of ridicule and misunderstanding.

Day after day, her questions churned inside her. Finally, no longer able keep to her concerns to herself, she confided in Paul, her husband. After many late-night conversations, she knew what she needed to do. In a bold move, Maaianne left the company. She and Paul packed up their goods and their children, left South Africa, and headed home to her roots in Kufunda, a small village in Zimbabwe. Maaianne had arrived at "ground zero," with no way of describing her inner void to anyone. Clearly, an era of her life had ended.

Every woman's endings have their own factors and textures. Perhaps you are being ushered into a life transition by gnawing dissatisfaction, restlessness, depression, or a lack of integrity—not unlike the inner disturbance that Maaianne experienced. The realization of discontinuity between what you are doing and who you are becoming on the inside may sneak up on you over time, until it breaks surface as an awareness that something needs to change.

Or you may face more sudden or jagged endings, triggered either by a deliberate choice on your part or external circumstances that shift. This kind of ending is often the result of the termination of an important relationship. Perhaps the organization you work for has downsized and you are asked to leave. Or a death or illness brings life as you have known it to a close. Whether an ending comes as a gradual realization that you have moved away from your inner truth, or as a sudden finale to how things have been for a long time, change is under way. In the period that follows an ending, you may notice a quiet lull or a blazing gap that opens between what has been and a new life that has, as yet, no distinct shape. All you can do is patiently navigate these uncharted waters.

Maaianne's new life was very simple: no goals, no timetables. She stripped down to home and family, she let go of images and responsibilities of global import. Having made the painful break with her past, she waited hopefully for the heavens to open up and a great voice to clearly announce her new path. But there was only silence . . . silence and mundane chores. Determined not to resolve the tension of not-knowing with some brilliant idea about a big new life-purpose, Maaianne courageously chose the void. Ideas were easy enough to come by—instead, she would hold out for a call from deep within.

For two years, Maaianne passed her days engaged in simple routines with the community of twenty-eight adults and children who lived in Kufunda. Eventually she forgot she was listening for anything, and just lived from day to day. She slowed down and relaxed into the rhythms of village life and what she described as a "new quality of being." The community studied permaculture together and, over time, turned the sandy soil into a lush garden at the center of their community. Maaianne happily made soap, and spent time in the bush studying local medicinal herbs with the other women. She valued their inner wealth and wisdom, and their skill at working so adeptly with what they had. Working side by side with these friends, she participated in storytelling that helped the women build confidence and find their own voices, in their marriages and in village affairs. To Maaianne's surprise, the immediacy of her simplified life took on a gentle beauty and a quality of magic. In these years, she and Paul often talked about following their joys as stepping stones into the future.

Maaianne's experience is a good example of the "in-between phase" that can follow an ending. Familiar territory has disappeared, and a new direction has not yet shown itself. Lingering in this "unknown land" can be unsettling for many of us. And unlike Maaianne's husband, who was willing to ride the unknown with her, those who want to support us may be even more unsettled than we are, especially if they have not themselves developed a relationship with such hiatuses from purposeful action. They may ask, "What do you plan to do next?," and will likely be unnerved if you answer, "Right now, nothing," or "I'm listening for my calling," or "I'm cleaning out some old baggage." Sincere family and friends often want to repackage us in a way that they understand—and as soon as possible.

Despite pressure to get on with it, conscious waiting and patience, as Maaianne demonstrates, are the order of the day—or month, or year, or however long it takes for new ground to firm up under you. The work in this open-ended period of listening and reflection is to slow down, let your cells reconfigure, and heal your heart. You are clearing the necessary space in which new impulses can arise from deep within to reshape your life. These impulses are the stirrings of new beginnings that already lie in wait.

The graceful movement through her days began to feel to Maaianne like a dance . . . so much so that she began to literally dance. Every day, she carved out an hour to simply move in the new rhythm and energy that she felt. For one month, Maaianne experimented with free-form dancing for that hour each day. The "yes" in her body led to a promise to herself to dance for an hour for each of 100 more days . . . which evolved into a commitment to a thousand days . . . and, eventually, a transformed life. Maaianne loosened and lightened, and now reports "coming home to a central part of myself." The exhaustion she had felt when she first arrived in Zimbabwe had gradually transformed into an energized flow that was leading her somewhere important for her soul's journey. For a long time she couldn't name that direction, but she felt it in the quickening in her body. Eventually, it dawned on her that the healing and freedom she was finding in her movement might now be her gift to a wider community of women.

Synchronistically, while discovering dance on her own, Maaianne learned of the school of Movement Medicine, a dance form that was being taught in the UK. Feeling immediately drawn to it, her heart leapt with joy. A new directive seemed to be organizing her life.

As Maaianne befriended her own not-knowing, she found the patience to wait, to listen to what was arising in herself, and to yield to a simpler life. In those seemingly fallow years lay dormant the potential that would shape a new era of her life. For Maaianne, that potential was dance. What is it for you? Have you slowed down enough to hear what is gathering, just out of sight? Might it be something brand new, or a new version of familiar thread? Do certain images or inclinations recur over and over for you?

Such ideas or inclinations may continue to simmer over time and are worthy of exploration. Careful discernment is needed to make sure that the possibilities that attract you are indeed the call of your soul, rather than a response to the world's expectations of you. Over time, some options will begin to feel more substantial, and a more clearly defined direction will become apparent. Try them on—as Maaianne did with her step-by-step commitment to a daily dance practice. As you sense the quality of this direction and commit some time and energy to it, you may find that opportunities and ideas begin to appear that strengthen the possibility. Creative partnerships may show up to energize your life and fire your imagination. The excitement of healthy initiation prevails, and a new beginning is launched.

Now Maaianne knew what she wanted to do, but how? She had commitments to her family, and the training would cost more than they could afford, now that she had let go of her company. But she didn't let the questioning undermine her knowing. Once again, synchronicity stepped in. A gas company in Tanzania offered Paul an attractive leadership position that involved designing a prototype for ecological sustainability and community involvement. The job matched up precisely with Paul's longtime commitment to responsible development of natural resources in Africa, and Maaianne recognized the spark of "yes" in his eyes. Not only would this job serve Paul's calling, it would support the family and provide the needed assistance for Maaianne's dance training. Once they had let go of traditional images of family life, they arranged for Maaianne and the children to live half of the year in Tanzania with Paul, and the other half in their community in Zimbabwe where the children could attend a Waldorf kindergarten in a nearby city. Both locations allowed for Maaianne to travel as she needed to the UK while the children were being well cared for. "It was hard for Paul to leave the kids," Maaianne reflected, "but we've learned from our journeys that a happy Dad 50% of the time is far better than an unhappy Dad (or Mom) 100% of the time. We love our children, and wish to teach them the beauty and value of following our dreams."

I have witnessed, over and over, the way that life conspires to fulfill deeply sourced dreams. Maaianne was clearly on her destiny line, more vibrant than I had ever known her. The bonus was that when Paul yielded to an open-ended time of regrouping in Kufunda, a surprising new direction arose for him, too, one that was aligned with his values and career trajectory.

Once life signals a new direction that truly fits, perseverance and commitment are needed to piece everything together. Maaianne and Paul needed to figure out how their aspirations could work for the whole family. They had entered the phase I call Tending. For them, this meant developing a second home and friends in Tanzania while continuing to invest energy in their life in Zimbabwe. Maaianne remained active in the village, and maintained her support of a school, based on the Waldorf approach to education, which she had started in nearby Harare. She made sure all of her children's needs were covered when she traveled to the UK to study with her teachers. And every day, she continued to honor her commitment to dance. Maaianne's dedication over time represents the kind of constancy that Tending requires. The fruits of her persistence became evident when she decided to offer some dance classes in Harare. Women were drawn to Maaianne's passion, radiance, and growing expertise. "The medicine of the dance is already working its magic and will continue," she reported. "A new friend will take over the class when I am not around. It is beautiful."

Some commitments, such as remodeling a kitchen, require a relatively short-term concentration of energy to complete. Other endeavors require longer-term tending—

such as Marianne's two-year training program as a Movement Medicine teacher, and her long arc of devotion to parenting, which would extend over decades. It is not uncommon for women to tend multiple long-term commitments at the same time. When one of our commitments comes to its completion, whether it be a short- or a long-term endeavor, we come full circle to an ending.

Though Maaianne's life intensified when she answered the call to study Medicine Movement, and her home life stretched across Africa, she never deserted the fundamental rhythms of Being that she had found in her days in Kufunda. Her experience of peace in herself and attunement with the land on which they lived persisted as the foundations from which her dance, and in fact her whole life, subsequently flowed. She had found the core sense of Self that lived within her. I refer to this centering point as Being.

Though most of us don't have a literal village to return to that is synchronized with the rhythms of the seasons and celestial motion, we can deliberately slow down and attune to the ever-present quietude that lives beneath the intensities of life in the twenty-first century. This is especially important when we are in the midst of major transition. In this stillness we can remember who we are, and more easily recognize the subtle qualities and directives inherent in the invisible streaming wholeness that awaits entry into our lives.

Mapping Life Transitions

Marianne's story clearly moves through a *period of endings* (when some chapter of a life is closing), *in-between spaces* (between what has been and what is not yet manifest), *new beginnings* (when fresh options begin to surface), and a duration of *tending* (caring for what has been initiated). These phases are often interwoven, and we don't always go through them all in a neat sequence. But ultimately, the way we engage with each phase determines the degree to which we are able to move through the entire process and arrive at a life that is congruent with the abiding Self that lives within.

These four phases show up in unique ways in most healthy processes of change. Each phase has a particular dynamic requiring specific qualities of attention and learned practices. Each asks for a different inner focus and outer resources. My goal in *Coming Into Your Own: A Woman's Guide Through Life Transitions* is to help you identify these distinct phases so that you may engage each one consciously and with some modicum of grace. I call these phases Dwelling Places because we literally need to *live* in each one until we have thoroughly completed our stay there, and realized the essential part that each one plays. Short-changing any one of them may mean missing the adventure of a lifetime, otherwise known as your calling. Trying to skip a phase, or refusing to face the demands of your immediate circumstances, will likely separate you from the supportive flow of life and necessitate a course correction down the road. People typically have favorite transition stages—and those they prefer to skip or skirt. For example, some don't like to admit when a familiar part of their lives is over. Others love the excitement of new beginnings, but are less inclined to see things through to completion. Some will do anything to avoid extended periods of "not-knowing." This guide will help you recognize and welcome *all* the Dwelling Places along the way. And you will remember a fifth place of residence, The Dwelling Place of Being, that lies behind all the others.

In the following diagram, the Wheel of Change links and orders these five Dwelling Places, which are essential to most life transitions. A map is never the territory itself, particularly if it charts a human process, its weakness being a necessary oversimplification of nuance and complexity. But a map can help you locate where you are now, and know what steps to take from here.

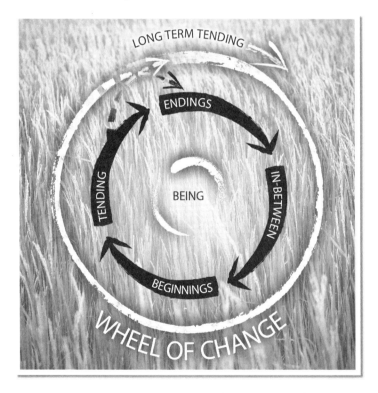

Here you see a cycle of personal transition that typically involves an *Ending*, followed by a period of time *In-Between*. Continuing clockwise, you see the eventual emergence of a *New Beginning*, and then the need for *Tending* that which has been initiated. Tending can be a phase that is completed in a relatively short span of time, or the sort of long-term commitment indicated by the movement in the outer circle. At the center is that abiding sense of Self, referred to as *Being*, which remains constant as the kaleidoscope of life continues to revolve around it.

The Field of Possibility for Your Life

The Wheel of Change rests on a field of grass that represents all of the unmanifested possibilities of your future. I call this your life's Field of Possibility. The field might hold a fiery presence that you have yet to express. It might contain an entrepreneurial propensity that you haven't yet tapped into. It might hold a quality of leadership that has waited for the right conditions to flower—or an artistic ability that has been invisible behind years of external service. Perhaps innate instincts for being a healer are seeking an outlet. The potential of motherhood may be alive in this field. Maaianne's Field of Possibility held her future as a dancer. I believe that we are here on earth to recognize and express the inherent potential that lives in this fertile field, awaiting particular expression at specific times in our lives.

Physicist David Bohm describes this potential as an "implicate order" that gives rise to the observable story of our lives. An important part of Bohm's work is the understanding that this enfolded potential is not a static blueprint. It is, in Bohm's terms, an "undivided wholeness in flowing movement." When this wholeness is streaming through you, you experience yourself in a meaningful flow. Each phase of the creative process described in the Wheel of Change is designed to connect you to this flow.

Other writers have different language for the same undivided reality. In his book *A Hidden Wholeness: The Journey Toward an Undivided Life*, Parker Palmer speaks about walking a path that is in alignment with your inner truth. Your internal reality, in his terms, is a combination of a personal ethic and your own unique potential. Expressing yourself with integrity in accord with these interior markers—despite the forces in the world that would have you betray your values, your sense of timing, your own feeling of "rightness"—leads to an undivided life. In my terms, this integrity is the congruency between your lived experience and the Field of Possibility.

A good metaphor for how the Field of Possibility gives rise to your unique expression can be seen in the miraculous journey of a caterpillar in becoming a butterfly. Embedded in the caterpillar is the blueprint for the future butterfly (its own template for its implicate order). After the caterpillar hardens its skin to form the protective encasement called a cocoon, its former structure dissolves into an undifferentiated mass of gelatin, except for several tiny "imaginal discs" that carry the design for the butterfly. These discs are not unlike stem cells. They have lain dormant, controlled by juvenile hormones that have held them in an inactive state. The trauma of the transformational process signals a decrease in these hormones, thus activating the pattern for a new stage of life—the butterfly. A latent organizing force is set in motion, supported now by a mature hormone. The Field of Possibility informs our own lives, not unlike our own "imaginal discs" that inform our dissolution and re-creation, time and again. We might say that our imaginal discs are the latent possibilities that wait inside us for the conditions that allow them to transform our lives.

If you are in the midst of transition, you can either strain to return to business as usual after the dust settles, or you can listen to your soul's transformative call embedded in the Field of Possibility. In the following chapters, the signs and symptoms of each of the Dwelling Places will be described in various ways, to help you find your current position on the Wheel of Change. The resources and practices at the end of each chapter will support you in fully occupying each Dwelling Place along the way, no matter how uncomfortable it is. The Appendices direct you to further resources that will be helpful and encouraging at critical junctures. Once you get your bearings, you will be able to sink into the requirements, challenges, and gifts of whatever Dwelling Place you might be residing in.

Seeing a cycle of deep transformation through to its completion will yield stronger faith that the support of life itself can be depended on. If the Wheel of Change were a three-dimensional model and we were looking at it from a side view, we would see it not as a flat repeating circle, but as an ascending spiral. From this perspective, each time we come into an ending cycle, for example, we would enter that territory with the benefit of successful previous experience at a lower rung on the spiral. Each time we complete one circuit of this spiral of creative process, we gain a deeper feel for its overall pattern. We become more confident that our feelings of "falling apart," and the experience of emptiness that often follows, are parts of a wholesome process as we await subtle guidance from the Field of Possibility. Coming to trust this hidden support is life-changing. We become wiser, more able to flow with the turbulent feelings and the apparent lack of control that arise in the process of transformation.

lonely

terrified

liberated

relieved

destabilized

raw

vulnerable

exposed

sorry

grief-stricken

humbled

pruned back

scared

anxious

depressed

2

The Dwelling Place of Endings: In My End Is My Beginning

We must be still and still moving
Into another intensity
For a further union, a deeper communion
Through the dark cold and the empty desolation,
The wave cry, the wind cry, the vast waters
Of the petrel and the porpoise.
In my end is my beginning.

T.S. ELIOT, FROM *THE FOUR QUARTETS*: "EAST COKER"

The end of a relationship, an accident, the death of a loved one, the end of health as we have known it, menopause, an emptying nest, retiring, loss of a financial base, moving out of a home, being laid off—all are entry ways into the Dwelling Place of Endings. Each alters the way we fit into our families; each changes our self-image and the future we have imagined. Well-known terrain, familiar habits, and guideposts disappear. All endings ask us to shed certain "givens," some of them blissful aspects of our lives that we have counted on; sometimes, they are more like old shoes that have become too tight as we have grown. Regardless of what our ending story is, the habits and familiar daily experiences that have defined and comforted us are likely being peeled away.

Endings are inevitable in all of our storylines as they weave through cycles of forming and dissolving. When a chapter of life ends, we often find ourselves in a vortex, swirling in various levels of terror, vulnerability, denial, grief, and, possibly, relief. Endings loom large in our memories as we look back over our lives. Many of us remember how we felt when our first love came to an end, and what it took to trust again. Whether the ending is welcomed or mourned, how we handle closure affects the ongoing quality and course of our lives, and often shapes our future choices.

The biggest challenge in navigating an ending may be letting go of our imagined control over our future. *If I let go of control, will my life fall apart? Is there* really *an organizing force working to reorder my life and bring me closer to my destiny? Could life possibly be presenting a threshold that will give me access to my potential?*

When a phase of life ends, we may be required to let go of a host of associated beliefs about ourselves and the world. *Maybe I am not the together, in-charge person that I have presented to the world. Maybe the experts don't have any idea what is right for me. Maybe I am not invincible. Maybe I have a right to be happy.* Facing an alternative reality can feel liberating, but it is not unusual that the stripping away required to enter that reality comes with feelings of fear, failure, grief, or shame.

Despite the messiness, sadness, and unknown consequences of endings, I suspect that most of us would choose a definite closure rather than permanent blisters on our feet from those shoes we've outgrown. As destabilizing as endings can be, they are also an invitation into a new relationship with life.

One day, the voice of change deep down inside us begins gaining strength, saying—first in a whisper, and eventually as a loud, clear challenge—"Leap." You take the leap when enough layers of resistance have loosened their grip, when the timing in your unique journey is right. Anxiety, repeated illness, low energy, informative dreams—you have passed through some of these to arrive at the edge of the precipice, ready to go jump. There you stand, in the light of realization, knowing that some part of your life is behind you.

Listening to Our Bodies

In my life, clarity about endings has repeatedly followed accidents of my own making that conveyed information about the need for change. Often my body was the messenger. Freshly out of graduate school, I took a job teaching at the University of California, Davis. During my first quarter I felt a disturbing lack of confidence, and gradually realized that I was uneasy presenting material that I didn't know firsthand. For the most part, my authority in the classroom was based on what I had studied, not on what I had lived. I remember that, behind my degrees and my professional role, I felt hollow, like an imposter. Following a failed attempt to alter my job in a way that would allow me to teach more authentically, I quit. Nothing seemed to fit any longer—first my job, and on top of that my marriage felt like it was missing dimensions that were important to me.

My husband had just received a consulting contract with the armed forces at a top-secret military base in Montana. I remember the sick feeling in my stomach one crisp fall day, when we passed through the checkpoint and drove into the compound. Looking back, I realize that it would have been very wise of me to heed that sense of foreboding. My discomfort with the role of Military Wife overlaid the widening gap between my husband and me that I was too afraid to admit.

A week after our arrival, I put a pot of beans on the stove and decided to go shopping while they were cooking. I turned the flame up high to get the water boiling and left for the grocery store, but forgot to turn the burner down to simmer. Halfway along the potato-chip aisle, I remembered. Overcome with panic, I ditched my cart and drove madly home, to find a fire truck in front of our apartment, firemen, hoses in hand, spraying water through our windows. Apparently the beans had caught fire, and a spark had ignited the kitchen curtains, which then torched our apartment and the two officers' quarters on either side of us. Having seriously lost favor on the base—especially with the officers and their wives whose belongings had been thoroughly incinerated or smoke damaged—I decided it might be a good idea to leave. My husband agreed that it would be best if he finished out his contract without me present. We were both relieved when a job offer arrived for seasonal work at an outdoor education center in Canada. I left for the summer, assuming we'd reconnect several months later.

Not long after, that next summer while in the Canadian Rockies, I survived a near-death climbing accident in which I tumbled 1,500 feet over ice and rock. As I lay in a broken heap at the bottom of the ice field, two important thoughts crossed my mind. First, I was still alive. Then I laughed aloud, in utter surrender to the obvious need for a change of life direction. I said to myself, "Three strikes and you're out, Barbara, and you've had two." At last, I was paying attention. Later, in the hospital, recovering from the reconstruction of my jaw, I had a lot of time to think about what had happened and where I was now headed.

When the Canadian Climbing Association, which keeps detailed records of the causes of climbing accidents, asked me to file a report, I wrote that the incident was caused by my reluctance to end my marriage and face the need for a new direction in my life. Despite objections from friends and family who loved my husband and saw us as the ideal married couple, I set out into the unknown, single, following a dim light of promise.

I do not recommend serial accidents as a way to get the message through to yourself that something is over. One of my life lessons has been to practice early detection of an ending by listening more carefully to subtle indicators, especially those in my body. Having witnessed the transition processes of hundreds of women, I am convinced that our bodies often get the message that a relationship, a job, a life direction is over before our minds realize what is happening.

It is not uncommon for women to resist clearly seeing what is actually happening. Many of us are sincerely dedicated to, or doggedly insistent about, seeing a particular direction through, no matter what effect it is having on our emotional and/or physical health. For women, self-sacrifice is even held up as a virtue. In my case, accidents were life's way of getting my attention, but other common messengers are depression and autoimmune diseases. When we fail to read the early signals that indicate the need for an ending, physical challenges or emotional breakdowns appear as harbingers of that change.

Releasing Assumptions and Expectations

It is common to base our lives on ideal scenarios of what we want or expect. Sometimes these are conscious, and sometimes they are based on hidden assumptions. We imagine ourselves married until we die, or living to be 90 years old, or owning our own home. Some of these scenarios are the manifestation of our soul's calling, but often they are woven into cultural standards and values. Whatever the mix of inner and outer influences, we hold on to our image of the future and make choices according-ly. When our imagined scenario fails to materialize, our sense of who we are can unravel. Such junctures invite us to consciously examine those assumptions and the degree to which they align with our heart's calling.

This is what happened to Gina, the daughter of a very close friend of mine. Gina shared her story with me, hop-ing it might be helpful for other would-be mothers. It is a story about how hopes and expectations for a particular kind of future can evolve into an entirely unexpected reality.

A central part of the bond between Gina and her husband, Jason, was their dream of raising children together. Gina had had a rare form of cancer in her teens, and though she had fully recovered, the disease had made it difficult for her to conceive. She and Jason tried for eight years, to no avail. By this time Gina was in her thirties, and they decided to try in vitro fertilization (IVF).

They found a trustworthy doctor to oversee the long, complicated process. The drug treatment, injections, and expense were worth it to them, as they persisted in their shared dream of creating a family. The procedure yielded six fertilized eggs, two of which were implanted. One egg attached and began to grow. Jason and Gina were thrilled. Then she miscarried. Despite the deep waves of loss, sadness, and fatigue, they tried again, with the four remaining fertilized eggs. Gina failed to get pregnant, and their first cycle of IVF came to an end.

Gina told me about the defining moment when her vision of their future began to dissolve. One day, she opened her refrigerator and stood staring at the leftover drugs that she would use to begin her second cycle of IVF. At that moment, she distinctly and literally heard the voice of wisdom speak. A quiet, clear, internal voice simply said, "I don't need to do this." The effort was over. When she told Jason about it that night, he was supportive, fully aware of how taxing the IVF process had been, physically and emotionally. Together, they let go of their dream.

Gina applied to graduate school, partly as a way to shift her focus away from her grief. Throughout her first year of intense study, she regularly saw a therapist, who helped ease the layers of sorrow she carried. On graduating with a master's degree in education, she and Jason decided to explore the possibility of adoption. Aware of the potential complication with adoptions in the United States, they decided to request a child from another country. After tedious and lengthy negotiations with officials in China and Ethiopia, they were rejected due to Gina's former illness. When this second, modified dream of family was shattered, Gina entered another round of grieving. In the wake of her deep disappointment, she decided to give herself a three-month break from considering parenthood.

When she re-emerged, adoption in the U.S., despite the risks, was back on the table. Her therapist recommended a proven adoption attorney, and one year later, after several other possibilities had come and gone, they found a young mother who had chosen to give up her baby. With eagerness and trepidation, Gina and Jason went to meet Cara. All three of them were touched and surprised by the bond of heartfelt connection that was present. Again, their hopes rose. Then, six months into her pregnancy, Cara gave in to her parents' pressure and reversed her decision.

Again Gina and Jason were devastated, as this third version of their dream dissolved. And once more, all they could do was let go. A month later, Cara contacted them again. She had cleared up a misunderstanding with her mother, who now supported her decision to release the baby. Were Gina and Jason still interested? They were amazed but unsure. Did this wavering foreshadow a life of reversals from the birth mother? Gina heard the same distinct inner voice. This time, it said, "Trust her." They did.

Cara invited Gina and Jason to be present at the birth, along with her own parents. For all of them, it was an occasion of love and wonder. As Gina left the hospital, carrying the baby in her arms, the final shreds of her dream to bear her own children slipped away forever. "I had in my arms the child that was mine, who was meant to be with us all along."

Now a mother, Gina looks back over that grueling nine-year process in which she and Jason peeled away, one by one, the layers of scenarios they had imagined. She knows that everything in this story, all the way back to her cancer, had paved the way for this particular human being to find her and Jason so they could share their lives together. In gratitude, they named their daughter Grace.

Our deepest intent links us to the Field of Possibility that holds our potential. Of course, each of us imagines our own version of *how* our intentions will unfold, but, like Gina and Jason, we may have to let go of these imagined agendas again and again as we bow to circumstances and continually open to what life gives us. What looks like an ending may actually be an opening into the very circumstance that has been waiting to unfold.

Letting Go, Facing Facts and Feelings

The hallmark of endings is the need to let go of what has ended, whether it be the release of a self-image or of long-held dreams, as we saw with Gina—or of a circumstance that has defined your life, such as a special relationship. The ways we define ourselves rarely drop away without our resisting their disappearance.

At the threshold of letting go, fear often rears up. We fear the loss of something dear to us, or we fear hurting someone or being hurt ourselves. Perhaps we fear retribution or judgment if we make a change. Or we fear the unknown, sensing a looming emptiness beyond the letting go.

Letting go of a person or something in which we've invested our lifeblood is not easy, whether it be a child who is now leaving home, a favorite painting we have just sold, or retirement from a satisfying job. An ending may be accompanied by grief—or, if the ending implies failure, overwhelming shame. Anger is a common response to an ending that we didn't consciously choose.

It takes emotional maturity to look honestly at one's circumstances and deliberately move through the emotional intensity that can accompany an ending. At some point, as the ending looms before us, facing facts and feelings becomes more critical than preserving an image or maintaining control. Letting go becomes more important that suppressing painful emotions we don't want to feel. At this point, the danger of holding on becomes greater than the risk of letting go, lest you pass by the moment of opportunity when the ending can most practically and gracefully occur. Missing this moment can send you through another round of living, only to end up at the same choice point.

Zeynep (*ZAY-nep*) was a senior executive in the Turkish office of a multinational corporation. When the pressures of her successful career became too much to bear, she walked courageously into this choice point. Living in Istanbul, a city situated on the border where Europe becomes the Near East, Zeynep herself embodies the opportunities and struggles of living at the confluence of two worlds. On the western side of the Bosporus Strait, which cuts the city in half, are modern art museums, Christian churches, and throngs of students in the streets demanding reform. When you cross the bridges to the eastern side, you are overcome by the complex smells of the spice market, the towering Blue Mosque, and the insistence of carpet vendors. Hundreds of minarets pierce the skyline, adorned with loudspeakers that transmit the chants of the imams calling Muslims to prayer five times a day. On the west side, nightlife throbs till 2 AM seven days a week; on the east side, shops, restaurants, and the few bars close by 9 PM. Straddling both worlds, Zeynep dresses in stylish Western apparel, yet the blessings and challenges of her Eastern heritage live within her.

Because Zeynep was the sole woman leader among the legion of men in her corporation, and her every move was seen to represent "all women"—she dared not under-achieve. This motivation dovetailed with an obsession with perfection that she had developed early in life. However, being perfect in her work meant that her young daughters and the husband she adored were neglected because of her long work hours. The dilemma contributed to serious mental, emotional, and physical strain.

By the time Zeynep sought refuge in a CIYO course in Istanbul, she was bone tired and quaking, with no choice left but to let go of an impossible balancing act. She walked

cautiously into the unfamiliarity of a women's circle, unsure of its ability to hold her pain and confusion. She was
surprised by the candor of the other women present, and
immediately felt their genuine care and trustworthiness.
She had found a place where she could let go of control
and break down without fear of judgment. At the end of
the four-day course, her aversion to fundamental change
had been trumped by the imperative of the truth. Zeynep
knew that she had reached the end of the lifestyle she had
created.

The morning after returning home from the course,
Zeynep submitted a letter to her supervisor requesting a
sabbatical, a step so unprecedented in her work culture
that he had to look up the meaning of the word. In her
letter, despite knowing that the action would likely cost
her her job, Zeynep was honest about her physical and
mental state. At that point, self-preservation was her only
concern. Her request triggered consternation from senior
leaders in the company, but also the admiration of colleagues, who felt their own need for respite from 70-hour
work weeks.

At a point of true completion such as Zeynep's, the risk
of losing what has long been so important pales before the
risks involved in not speaking the truth. She had to risk
everything for the sake of greater health and wholeness in
her life. Much to Zeynep's surprise, instead of firing her,
her supervisor offered her six months' paid leave.

During this hiatus from work, Zeynep worked with
a therapist to revisit the childhood experiences that had
produced in her a standard of perfection that ultimately

threatened her wellbeing. She gave herself the gift of bodywork to release the severe physical tension that had built up in her body from decades of stress. She developed new rhythms with her family, and spent healing time alone by the Mediterranean Sea.

At the end of her six months of sabbatical, Zeynep felt centered and calm, and had opened to the idea of finding another career. But again her boss surprised her, this time offering her a new position in the company, with even more responsibility and seniority than her former job had required. After seriously pondering the option, Zeynep realized that the real ending that had occurred in the last six months was not her termination of work at the company, but the letting go of *the way she had been working*—that is, her motives and habits around perfectionism, her need for control, and the exceptionally high standards she held herself to.

Zeynep returned to the corporation committed to a new way of living and working. First of all, she substantially cut back the number of hours she worked and made her family's needs a higher priority. She practiced forgiving imperfections in herself and in her employees. She let go of her habit of forcing things to happen, and instead acknowledged that directions suggested by others that were in contradiction to her own ideas often had validity. No longer repressing her own feelings or insights at home or at work, Zeynep has learned to speak up in a non-blaming way. Her habit of saying "yes" to every request of her has been tempered with easy "nos." The top priority in her life became the preservation of an inner equilibrium.

Facing the End of a Marriage

Zeynep's willingness to face the facts and her feelings took great courage, but ultimately, facing her untenable reality led her to a healthier, happier life. Dealing with relationships that have become untenable requires the same kind of courage and a keen sense of timing. In this realm particularly, avoiding the perceptions and intuitions that speak to us of an ending can make a healthy readjustment more agonizing in the long run.

Social conventions traditionally frame marriage as a binding contract until death. From this "death do us part" perspective, it can be hard to accept changes that affect that original contract and the expectations explicit in it. As a result we can overstay the actual ending of a relationship cycle, unwilling to admit the truth and consent to the consequences. However, persistence beyond the point of a healthy ending often erodes civility in a couple and unconsciously triggers ugly interactions that then become the ostensible justification for the separation. The parties involved end up assuming that the relationship is coming to an end because of the destructive exchanges rather than recognizing that the initial loving connection has evolved into a different form of relationship. However, when two hearts are involved it can take a while for both to accept the end, especially the one who has not initiated the change.

There is a delicate line between determining whether a relationship itself has come to an end, or instead some aspect of it is needing to grow or change, as was true for Zeynep when she had to change *how* she did her job.

Perceiving the difference can be challenging. But rather than employing of avoidance tactics, being honest with one's self and then with one's partner is the best way forward, often requiring the help of an impartial counselor. Disregarding intuition that speaks to us of an ending can have painful and complicated repercussions. I know of young couples that have tried to fix a broken relationship by having a baby as a way of strengthening their bond. Most often this "solution" delays an inevitable parting, with major impact on the child. Some husbands or wives seek to relieve the pressure of an incompleteness in their marriage by finding a parallel relationship that is more satisfying, temporarily muting the facts and feelings about the state of the marriage. If secrecy is involved, connection to the Field of Possibility is clouded, making it hard to perceive the real nature of the relationship and what steps can be taken to shift into this arrangement. Secrecy only delays the honest conversations needed to explore forward movement in the most respectful and healthy ways possible. This being said, I note that some couples negotiate the terrain of multiple relationships in transparent and wholesome ways that redefine what marriage is for them.

As difficult as it may be, recognizing an ending in a timely way and naming its conclusion open the way for a more amicable completion and less suffering for all involved. If we disregard the signs that tell us a relationship is over, it can take a serious breakdown to force us to let go of this fundamental structure in our lives and the beliefs and assumptions that have held it in place. As we pay increasing attention to disconnection between our outer choices and our inner knowing, we become more sensitive to early signs of divergence. Doing the inner work needed to understand our part in this bifurcation allows us to speak what is true for us, to say what we expect and need, to voice what we can't tolerate—and at the same time listen respectfully to the same from our partners. As we dedicate ourselves, over time, to this kind of self-reflection, authenticity, and integrity, cellular memory of positive outcomes accumulates. And we'll have built the internal solidity necessary to part ways, if that is the right result. Learning to show up in our truth and live with all that this sets in motion, we come to trust that new life will flow into the voids—bringing with it a new direction, perspective, and identity that is increasingly aligned with our core Self.

Grieving as a Rite of Passage

Endings, whether sudden or gradual, self-chosen or happenstance, are often accompanied by a process of profound grieving. Grief is a journey that requires patience, support, and trust in a cycle of mourning that has its own rhythms and longevity. It invites you into the depths of yourself, and into a private intimacy with life's mystery.

For decades, my commitment to helping women live more authentic lives has paralleled the work of colleague and friend Suzanne Anderson, who runs leadership programs for women. (See Appendices: Further Resources). Her husband, David, started the first coffee-cart business in Seattle, which inspired the drive-in coffee chains that have become so popular in the United States. But hidden beneath David's brilliant entrepreneurial spirit were private demons and a health crisis that few people knew of, not even his wife. When David unexpectedly took his life, Suzanne was left stunned and devastated. The waters of grief poured from her eyes and heart in great rivers as her life disintegrated around her. She faced layer after layer of realization and implication as she came to terms with the suicide and loss of her beloved, and a devastating trail of unfinished business David had left behind. Because of the deep transformative work she had done with women for many years, Suzanne knew how important it was to face the reality of what happened, and to accept everything that arose in her.

Soon after David's death, Suzanne eked out a few words to me about her experience of this ending in her life. I share these words with her blessing, in deep respect:

> It is hard to believe that it was only seven weeks ago that my life changed so dramatically when I heard the impossible words "David is dead," and the bottom fell out of my world. His sudden and chosen death has devastated the way I have known myself . . . and the future I imagined ahead was cleaved away like a giant iceberg breaking free. And here I am now . . . on the edge of a new and unimaginable chasm.

> It has been a descent like no other. I am being unraveled at the deepest level, and the vessel of my life as I knew it has been harshly shattered like a pottery vase on a cold stone hearth. It is also a tender time . . . with waves of grief, fear, anger, joy, despair . . . and the healing comes by making room for all this to happen. Which I am doing, one moment at a time.

Our endings may not be as severe and heartbreaking as Suzanne's, but they may contain some aspects of the raw grief she describes. A friend of mine calls grief a watercourse that flows as it will, going underground and resurfacing. Our tears are tributaries of that stream, which eventually finds its way to the sea. Western cultures try to engineer a channel for this natural river of grief. A small window of time in which to fall apart is considered acceptable, but soon after, the pressure to "move on" mounts. There is scant understanding that the river of grief has its own timing, and takes a unique, wandering course for each person and each situation.

To move on into a new life, we must honor our own particular way of grieving. My niece, Marin, was 22 years old, a budding artist at a college in Maine, when her father was diagnosed with brain cancer. Wesley was a dean at the Fuqua School of Business, in his mid-forties and a strong candidate for Provost at Duke University. Marin refused to accept her father's diagnosis, and held fiercely to her hope for his recovery. In her mind, she imagined the tumor as a butterfly in her father's head that would one day fly away. Over and over, for two years, Marin painted the butterfly as a way of keeping her father alive. She was devastated when the unimaginable happened.

After my brother's death, Marin made it through graduation by sheer willpower, pushing her grief aside as best she could. When the space finally opened for her to collapse, she went back to the North Carolina home where she and her father had spent many happy years together. Determined to hold on to her memories of him, she buried herself in his letters. As Marin read through them, a vision came to her of an art project that would allow her to "be" with her father and honor the great person he was: she would make a quilt using the clothes that still hung in his closet. Marin searched for a context that could understand and support this process, and allow her to safely fall apart as she literally stitched her memories together.

Marin located a textile course at Penland College, in the nearby Smoky Mountains. She gathered up her father's old, soft work shirts, some with ticket stubs to basketball games still in the pockets, folded them into his suitcase, and headed for the mountains. Unable to afford enrollment as a full-time student, she registered as a "local" and camped in a field near the school. It was a lonely and pivotal time in her life.

Marin cut the shirts into patches and carefully pieced them back together. "I wanted to create a monument in the world that was worthy of his presence," she reflects. Stitch by stitch, she dismantled her anger and sadness, weeping without reserve. In the end, she didn't produce a monumental piece of art. More importantly, she had faithfully followed her own watercourse, which told her where to go and what to do in order to process her grief.

Marin left the mountains with a lighter heart, more able to function in the world and withstand the stream of grief that would continue to flow over time. By trusting her own instincts, she had discovered new ground in herself on which to weather the ebbs and flows of life.

Some women who grieve may not have the luxury to go on a retreat, as Marin was able to do. They may need to return to work midway through a grieving cycle. I suggest that they go about their day-to-day responsibilities while deliberately easing back on their emotional involvement in normal demands. Finding a more neutral stance relative to all the ups and downs of your job helps to protect the heart and maintain space for the delicate underlying process under way. Sometimes, grieving lasts for years; quietly, we must find ways to honor that span as we go about living and loving.

In the end, grieving ushers out an era and makes room for a new life. For much of my life, I didn't recognize sadness until it had collected, like water in an over-filled lake. When the strain to contain the water became greater than my efforts to maintain composure, a dam would break, releasing a flood of tears that gushed through many layers of unexpressed grief. After such a flood, I would notice that I could think more clearly. I found that the ensuing quietude inside me made me more sensitive to adjustments needed in my life. And my sponged-out heart had more space in it for giving and receiving love.

I have learned that, in addition to our personal journeys, this alchemy is applicable on a collective basis. As I write this book in 2014, I am aware of the humanly created stress on the planet that will affect the lives of our children and our children's children. As women, we can't come into our own without finding a healthy response to the challenges we face regarding the health of this earth. Our paths into the future are being affected by the threats to civility, environmental devastation, and economic instability. For years, massive grief about the possible loss of the livability in our common home lay beneath the surface of my feelings, making it difficult for me to find my stance in the face of the overwhelming implications.

In 2014, I attended a workshop with author and environmental activist Joanna Macy in which we were invited to access the deep feelings we harbored about the future. Grief, anger, fear, and feelings of helplessness poured into the ritual space that Joanna had carefully prepared. We cried, raged, trembled, and dissolved in despair. We faced the possibility of failure. Three hours later, when the process had come to completion, I noted in the group the same kind of collective clarity that I personally feel when accumulated grief at last moves through me. I witnessed the unreserved expression of shared grief open a channel of awareness into the Field of Possibility that lies beneath the specter of impending global collapse. New possibilities arose, and each person began to discern the specific part she or he might play in this. I felt a particular calling clarify in myself, along with an unexpected surge of energy that has persisted to this day. I was thoroughly surprised that a wholehearted expression of collective grief could unleash the magnitude of gratitude, joy, creativity, and lightness of spirit that spread through that room.

In *Letters to a Young Poet*, the German poet Rainer Maria Rilke writes about sadness as a particular doorway into the future:

> We can't say who has come, perhaps we will never know, but many signs indicate that the future enters us in this way in order to be transformed in us, long before it happens. . . . The quieter we are, the more patient and open in our sadness, the more deeply and serenely the new presence can enter us, and the more we can make it our own.

As Rilke suggests, the grieving process is a rite of passage in which the seeds of the future are planted in the soil of our being and watered by our tears. As we grieve the passing of an "old life," our porous heart can perceive more easily the future that is ours, held in the Field of Possibility.

Making Peace with Death

In 2011, I was diagnosed with cancer. What should have been a simple surgical solution to the early stages of uterine cancer turned into a long and complicated challenge. The surgeon expanded the uterus with pressurized water to perform a test, then accidentally perforated the wall of my uterus with her instrument. The water escaped into my abdominal cavity, risking the spread of abnormal cells.

At first, when I found out what happened, I railed against God: I was too young, had too much yet to give, etc. People told me I had good grounds to sue the doctor. When the oncologist started to design the protocol for a year of chemotherapy treatment, I realized I was face to face with life and death. I would not know for at least a year whether the cancer had spread, as the cell multiplication would be too minute to detect. If it had spread, by the time it was detectable it would be Stage Four and untreatable. At this point I became acutely aware of our culture's assumption that death was "bad," or a failure of the medical system, or even a personal failure—something to be avoided at all costs.

I slowed down to consult my body. I weeded out what was relevant for me in the tidal wave of advice and information about cancer that flooded over me. In the end, I rejected the oncologist's recommendation of chemotherapy and instead opted for a year of waiting and seeing.

Having chosen to reject chemo, I squarely faced the possibility of terminal cancer. I gave up obsessing about whether this should or should not have happened and whose fault it was, accepted the implications of my choice, and—much to my surprise—experienced a profound sense of liberation. When I got right down to it, I was much more excited about living a life—even if it was a shorter life—that mirrored my inner guidance system than following someone else's recommendations, which might or might not prolong that life. This gripping adventure was far more interesting to me than survival.

I made an agreement with myself: I would take responsibility for my own healing. I worked to build my immune system to its maximum strength so that my body could deal with the proliferation of abnormal cells. I changed my diet and exercised regularly. I canceled travel plans. I relished time alone and in my art studio, and I saw only friends who were sensitive to my inner process and the quietness I craved.

A year later, I was blessed with good news. The scans came back clean.

I honor the difficult and unique decision-making process that each woman faced with cancer makes. I realized that I, in this circumstance, had learned to walk the path of sensitive listening to my inner directives, and to embrace them with the curiosity and courage necessary to follow the course they indicated—come what may.

Developing loyalty to the voice of my own guidance had a ripple effect on other parts of my life. One of those ripples went all the way back to my childhood. I remembered the shame I felt in my early years in the face of the stern refrain repeated by my parents: "Don't be selfish." The threat of their rejection of me when I put myself first felt to my young psyche like a fear of death; at the same time, I was so spitting mad at them that I figured out ways to appear compliant while constructing a secret life that gave me what I wanted. The result was decades of making choices that placed service to others above my own needs and justified overriding of my inner guidance. And at the same time, I became a chameleon, shifting my colors to stay in good favor with my parents while getting what I wanted on the sly.

But that year following my surgery had forced me to prioritize my own needs. I had walked straight into my fear that "shameless" tending to my own emotional needs would jeopardize my place in the family. I realized that giving to others and performing for others had become ways of buying their love. It took a leap of faith for me to test my value and connections to those I loved on the simple merit of who I was. As hard as it was for me, I canceled work engagements with people who were counting on me. Every time I said no, I had to choose again my newfound dedication to prioritizing my personal needs. Choosing rest over selfless service felt as if it would lead to a life-threatening exclusion from others. In fact, a number of friends *did* disappear during this time—I was surprised at who stayed with me when other, "closer" friends were nowhere to be seen. A new platform of friendship slowly formed.

When I legitimized my needs to myself and stood up unapologetically on this ground, the necessity for a hidden life at long last dissolved. Throughout that year, standing on the edge of the unknown, I would awaken to a more profound and unified sense of Self.

Shortly after the botched surgery, I came across poet Robert Frost's well-known words: "Two roads diverged in a wood, and I—I took the one less travelled by, and that has made all the difference." To this day, those lines live over my desk. Looking back, I would not forgo this situation. Recognizing and facing death gave rise to a fierce devotion to an authentic life. This episode was a small price to pay for the close partnership I now have with the wise dictates of my own knowing. My self-worth is no longer built around loyalty and the constant demonstration of my dependability, but rather it is commensurate with my ability to follow an inner directive. Sometimes when I wake at night, I curl up with my arms around my own body, happily providing the love and acceptance for myself that I formerly sought from others. The possibility of the ultimate ending triggered one of the most significant beginnings of my life.

Endings often don't seem fair or justified. A voice inside may say, "This should never have happened." If we keep telling ourselves that we've been "badly done by," we remain a victim of circumstances, and may miss a thread of value woven deeper in. A particular turn of events may even be a necessary way station on a journey to wholeness. Opening to the reality of *what is* can shift us out of insisting that we need ideal circumstances to make us happy, and into an appreciation of the growth that is called out of us by life's trials.

When we feel cornered by seemingly unjust endings, it can help to ask, "If I and the Universe (or your own word for a higher power) had conspired to create this situation exactly as it is in order for me to learn something vital at this stage in my journey, what might that lesson be? How might this realization serve the next phase of my life?" The answers that arise may surprise you. This practice can help us to remember and respect the journey to greater wholeness that is at work beneath the challenges and endings we face.

When Multiple Endings Converge

Sometimes we come to particularly intense junctures in our lives, where the Dwelling Place of Endings is crowded with multiple closures converging all at once. This could be a confluence of health challenges, jagged relationship changes, the need to move out of a home, a death in the family . . . or any other ending that, all on its own, would be experienced as significant. If this describes your current transition, I suspect that you are at a pivotal point in a spiritual journey in which your fundamental sense of Self is reconfiguring. What remains after this journey, when all else is stripped away, is nothing less than a wholeness from which a new consciousness and a new life can emerge. That's a reassuring promise, but when you are in the midst of the process it can feel like utter chaos.

It is critical that you do whatever you can to find the strong support of worthy counselors, coaches, friends, or family. The best supporters are those who understand that, as painful as it might be, the stripping away is not "bad."

These blessed companions don't try to fix things so that we feel better. They stand with us in the heat. They love us, and remain riveted on who it is that is emerging, no matter how disorienting and uncomfortable things get. They faithfully hold our hearts and maintain a steadiness as we waver and swing. Their precious gift is their knowing that the intensity we are feeling is a transformative fire that, in the end, is bringing us home to our immutable, radiant Selves. Honoring each moment of the passage may reveal more than we ever anticipated.

Joy in the Midst

We humans are sense-making beings. When something unexpected happens, we want to figure out why.

Myriads of books capitalize on this, telling us how to interpret a backache or a broken left rib, a car accident or a sudden reversal of fortune. Mining our circumstances for insights about the purpose of each situation yields a mental framework that may be temporarily comforting but ultimately confining. Mark Nepo, in his book *Seven Thousand Ways to Listen: Staying Close to What Is Sacred*, confounds our linear thinking when he says that trying to mentally make sense of things "assumes that experience is heading somewhere," whereas our heart sense presumes that living fully in the moment is the reward, and may not lead anywhere at all.

This is what my friend Sarah-Jane Menato has learned about making sense of her life. For more than thirty years, I have watched her grow through many challenges. Perhaps the stance from which she has faced these trials is what makes her a stellar coach and one of our most sensitive and perceptive CIYO guides (See Appendices: Further Resources). Sarah-Jane and I have found Nepo's book useful as a common reference when, together, we mull over our lives. From her home in England she wrote to me reflecting on how one of our favorite passages in *Seven Thousand Ways to Listen* has helped her receive endings that she would never have consciously chosen, as valued gifts. She chooses to open these gifts and put them to good use.

In his book, Nepo speaks about how, when giving his deep attention to some circumstance before him, great or small, a detail will touch and open him into a profound sense of meaning that is more a feeling than a mental construct. When this experience is brought in close to his heart, an unexpected intimacy with life opens to him— *the encounter itself is the meaning or gift.* He says that while *knowing* the truth about what and why something is occurring can lead to wisdom, simply *experiencing* the truth of how things are can lead to joy. "And while wisdom is helpful, joy is essential. While I can certainly live better with wisdom, even it becomes a burden to carry without joy."

One of the major endings Sarah-Jane had to contend with was her fight with the United States Immigration and Naturalization Service for the right to remain in the U.S. with her young daughter. Her loss of this battle resulted in a return to dysfunctional family dynamics and re-immersion in a culture she had hoped was behind her forever. Though she wouldn't have chosen these circumstances, she nevertheless accepted them, and eventually received gifts she never imagined, as her family worked through its challenges and she made peace with her roots. Later, with hindsight, Sarah-Jane could justify the move through interpretation of the turn of events in a positive way. In addition, and perhaps more importantly, she came to an entirely different way of being with the unique set of factors in her life. She writes:

> I feel that now, only now, at fifty-six years old, I am experiencing the joy that Mark Nepo is reaching to describe. All my adult life I have gained wisdom by making sense of my experience through watching, thinking, and writing. My interpretations were some-what stabilizing but also weighed me down. I am now having flashes of being able to release the weight of the hard-won wisdom without throwing out the substance. The courage to *feel and internalize* my experience, just as it is, is leading me to be able to taste the bittersweet of my life, and there is deep joy in that.
>
> Things rarely turn out well in my life or the lives of my coaching clients, *well* referring to the way we want them to turn out. I think that's what I'm in the process of learning. My joy, blessing, and fulfillment are in learning to stand on the ground that's uniquely my own, and engage it with my heart. This has little or nothing to do with the way things turn out.

I have admired Sarah-Jane's willingness to let her endings be as they are, to not need things to turn out "well" in order to experience joy. Resisting the impulses to deflect or complain about difficulties and injustices, she faces them with her gratitude for simply being here, regardless.

I have seen Sarah-Jane's appreciation for the greater life, in which her challenges flow and move, soften her pain and lead to profound moments of peace in the roughest of endings.

Lexi touched a similar experience. When her 18-year-old son left home, she felt devastated. Though it had been long anticipated, his actual departure threw Lexi into a well of sadness. She reached out to a circle of women friends via an e-mail that included a poem that sprang from her heart:

> I need to mark this moment, a powerful moment for our family. There is something about a son leaving home—hard to fathom until one gets here. Maybe especially when one's son is forging ahead on impulse with little safety net . . . kind of like his mama did before him. Here's my poem:
>
> My son left home yesterday.
>
> The usual: a clunky car, cheap sunglasses, and determination to follow a barely tangible thread.
> Up with him late the night before, listening to his crisis of faith—
> not enough money, fear of failure, so much uncertainty.
>
> Dammit, this is not the place I want him to go,
> not the tidy path I dreamed up for him.
>
> Yet I had to push him towards his dream
> knowing that following his path is the only way.

Today my mother task was to push past protective,
practical instinct
and pray that the Gods I raised him with
will follow along behind him
unoffended by exhaust fumes and untidy trail of
young promise.

Acknowledging and sharing the pain of this ending allowed Lexi to move forward in her life. Coming to terms
with this major transition would happen most deeply
through bringing the separation "close to heart," as Mark
Nepo puts it, and experiencing the joy of heart-wrenching
love for a son.

The endings we face may be unwanted and difficult,
yet the trauma and pain can lead us to a deeper connection
with life. We come into our own through many doorways.

Marking Endings

Speedy passage through endings without reflection or honesty with oneself—or without proper marking—can set up
a murky future. So it is important, as you leave the Dwelling
Place of Endings, to create an act of closure. Lexi's note to
carefully chosen friends is an example of a healthy way to
bless and mark an ending. This may be a private act of
completion, or it can include others who understand and
support your transition. The art of an authentic ritual to
mark an ending, as we saw with Marin's quilting in honor
of her father, helps us integrate deep loss into our ongoing
lives. These gestures also help those around us to adjust to
our changes and to support us in tender times.

In our culture we have baptisms, bar mitzvahs, and funerals—but how do we mark the less-celebrated passages that are also parts of our unfolding lives? What ceremony marks the end of a marriage? How do we leave a beloved country when life calls us to emigrate? How do we acknowledge the change in the quality of an established friendship when one party pulls back? How do we embrace the end of fertility when menopause arrives or a hysterectomy is required? How do we bless a miscarriage? What ritual marks the death of a dog or cat? How do we acknowledge with others the suicide of a friend?

Candidness about endings exposes vulnerability and feelings that many people find difficult to face. It takes courage to gather witnesses to embrace and honor a difficult ending. Such ceremonial acknowledgment, however, frees us to move into a new phase of life. When our current traditions fail to provide the template for marking a particular step on our journey, we are called on to create such a ritual. We might plan a ceremony that includes the company of others, or we may allow ourselves to be spontaneously drawn into a solo and solemn moment of farewell.

On the tenth anniversary of their relationship, Jude and her partner were given the gift of a plum tree by close friends. Together, early in the spring, they had selected the tree and planted it in the field in front of their home. A year later, their relationship ended. One day, about six months after they had split up, Jude was snowshoeing in that same field. Feeling drawn to the plum tree, she began circling it. Words came to her to speak aloud as she walked slowly round and round the tree.

I spoke about our love and partnership over the years, its blessings, and the strife, too. Sadness and gratitude intertwined, and I was comforted in the realization that the tree would live on as a symbol of our partnership, rooted in the land that we bought and tended together. That simple ritual helped me to honor and let go of who we were as a couple. I waded home through the white powder, the winter sun on my back, grateful that the fullness of what we had created in our years with one another lives on symbolically on this land.

Jude's spontaneous ritual was another layer of completion, helping her ease out of one era of her life and into the next.

I concluded my life-changing cancer saga by making gifts that carried the gratitude I felt for those who had supported me through four surgeries and a twelve-month vigil. For weeks I had considered the quality of this ending, reaching for a simple gesture that would ground my newfound relationship with my body, help me to weave myself back into the wider community after a year of retreat, and express my thankfulness. One day, the idea came to me to make herbal bundles for the women who had supported me. I asked Sahni Hamilton, an herbalist friend who specializes in healing ritual, to help me. (See Appendices: Further Resources.) I carefully chose nine healing herbs, including burdock, for its ability to help with worry about the unknown; oats, as a nervous-system tonic that soothes grief and loss; lavender, for its calming effect in the face of trauma; and holy basil, as the elixir of life. We wrapped them in antique lace from an old wedding dress, drawn to the porous, feminine quality of the hand-crafted tatting. Then we the placed each bundle in an outer pocket of earth-colored cotton. Finally, Sahni and I tied them with raffia and adorned them with wooden buttons and strips of astragalus, known for its help in adapting to change.

As a final touch I passed each bundle through the smoke of incense that I made from the resins weeping from fir trees that stand next to my home, and presented them to my "angels," along with a letter that honored the way they had held me. Some I delivered by hand, and others I sent to friends around the globe who have tracked me from afar. After making these bows to life and to cherished friends, I felt free to move on.

Endings have a way of dismantling our lives and self-images. Every ending and every season of grieving is a passageway that opens onto new ground. Each opens a hidden crack in the soil of Being in which the seeds of a distant and creative future can germinate. Thus, it is important to respect the cycles of endings as they pulse through us, on their own terms and in their own rhythms. Despite external pressure to return to "normal" when something ends, we need to protect all that naturally occurs in the heart.

Endings consciously faced and thoroughly integrated into our lives can lead to a liberating acceptance of life's circumstances, stronger faith in the continuous flow of life, and solid ground from which to take the next step on our soul's journey. Endings leave us changed. We are no longer the same person we were before, but who we are becoming is not yet clear. Unknowns loom. Most often, our next steps take us into the Dwelling Place of In-Between, where we must stay for a time . . . long enough for an invisible possibility to work its way into our awareness.

Helpful Practices in the Dwelling Place of Endings

Journaling

Journaling can be useful when you feel restless or uncomfortable in your current life situation, or when you are in the midst of realizing that something is over. Perhaps it is not completely obvious that a phase of your life is coming to an end. Perhaps you are resisting looking squarely and honestly at your current reality. Through journaling, your subconscious mind can speak and explore, unhindered by mental resistance. Because it provides an outlet for the thoughts and emotions cycling through you, journaling is a way to keep energy moving that might otherwise get knotted up.

Choose an inexpensive notebook in which to write, so that you feel free to pour out messy, free-form writing. Know that your writing is for your eyes only. Dismiss the part of you that judges your expression—in private journaling, there is nothing to accomplish. Some women use colored pencils; some sketch in the margins; some write in circles; others paste pictures onto the pages. Free yourself to follow whatever wants to be expressed in the safe alone time you have protected.

Weeks or months later, when you reread what you have written, you will likely learn something significant. Repeated patterns may become more evident. You may gain insights about where disturbances originate. You may notice cycles of highs and lows, and come to trust that you are not stuck in either extreme as life moves on. Your progress may become evident. Most important, you will have gained the vantage point of one who witnesses her own unfolding. This perspective can draw forth both generosity toward yourself and surprising wisdom.

In her book *The Artist's Way: A Spiritual Path to Higher Creativity*, which is written for the creative beings that we all are, Julia Cameron describes a journaling ritual she calls "the morning pages." She describes this process as a way of giving voice to a deeper knowing that lives within. Morning pages are three pages of long-hand, stream of consciousness writing done upon waking each day. She reminds us not to over-think our writing and says, "They are about anything and everything that crosses your mind. . . . Morning Pages provoke, clarify, comfort, cajole, prioritize and synchronize the day at hand."

Somewhere in the spontaneous mix of dreams remembered, fears unloaded, desires spoken aloud, requests for guidance, moaning, venting, and total nonsense come insights and the relief of having underlying truth put into words. Cameron quips that the morning pages should also be called "mourning pages," because in many ways they are "a farewell to life as you knew it and an introduction to life as it's going to be."

Asking for Support

As aspects of our lives collapse, we often feel ashamed and vulnerable. Life's circumstances may be too much for us to carry alone. But for many of us, the act of asking for help is a big step. Though it may be hard, this is an important part of successfully navigating your transition. Start by identifying a person or a small group of people you feel safe with, people who will not judge you in your raw state. I suggest that, as you negotiate an agreement that supports you in this fragile time, you deliberately move beyond an informal request. Ask for a focused conversation in which you discuss specifically how you want to relate.

Ask if your friend(s) are willing to stay with you for a particular duration of time, and decide together how you will communicate. It is important to tell your listeners precisely what you want from them, such as, "I need to sense my own way, but want a steadfast witness who will not try to fix me or give me advice." Or ask, "Can we set a time for a weekly call for the next three months?" Well-intentioned friends are inclined to try to make you feel better, but this may not be the neutrality you need. Their fundamental job is to keep seeing your inner gold and, no matter how chaotic things become, to love you for who you are. Be sure to discuss with them any concerns you have about confidentiality, making clear which of your words can or cannot be shared with others.

If you are experiencing intense grief, it may be useful to see if there is a grief support group in your town. Such circles, often facilitated by a grief counselor, can help navigate the psychological impacts and emotional waves that are natural parts of intense grieving.

Prayer

Prayer is another form of request for support. I don't mean prayer in only a religious sense. Whatever your beliefs, you can find comfort by reaching beyond yourself for help. This can involve conversing with a deity or another entity whom you believe supports your life. For example, I frequently visit a circle of oak trees that enfold and comfort me as they quietly receive my prayers. I imagine these oaks to be particular ancestors. I sit in the center of the circle, where I envision a mother tree once lived years ago who seeded the generation of surrounding trees. I speak my heart aloud to all of those present.

Prayer is a way of honoring a greater force in our lives. Even for those who are unsure about the existence of a supportive presence, an open-hearted request for help may be answered in some surprising way. In the spirit of humility, prayer can open the way for an impulse from the Field of Possibility that is beyond our ideas of what should or should not happen. In prayer, we honor the sacredness of life, in which we are gratefully included.

Finding a Life Coach or Therapist

It may be a significant step in your process to value yourself enough to seek professional help. Psychotherapists normally focus on the psychological obstacles to your forward movement. Life coaches usually concentrate on noticing what is ending and supporting what is beginning.

A trusted therapist or life coach never loses sight of your worthiness and innate wholeness. You are not a problem to be solved; rather, you are a unique person whose potential is being unlocked.

What you are looking for is someone who demonstrates keen insight about underlying causes of habits that no longer serve you, and who understands how to undo them. These professionals should not seek to impose their own suggestions or framework on you, but rather help you sense and define your own realization, direction, and perspective. Trust your instincts about who is a right fit for you.

There are great variations of ability and approach within both of these professions. Do some research before settling on someone to work with. You may want to speak to former clients of a therapist or coach you're considering working with to gain a better sense of their style and personality. Request the brief information meeting they typically offer. During and after this introductory conversation, consult first and foremost your intuition— and don't be afraid to move on if the relationship is not working in a way that feels constructive for you.

Caring for Your Body

During a stressful ending, it's particularly important to take care of your body. Exercise regularly to keep energy moving through your physical system. The amount of exercise you get is less important than its regularity. Stress is hard on the adrenals, so careful supplementation with herbs or vitamins that support healthy cortisol levels may ease the toll on your body. For example, a methylated B complex could be helpful for a fatigued nervous system.

When emotional pressures build, it can be helpful to have a safe method for releasing the intensity that builds up in your body. When I need to exert some energy in a controlled way, I find a punching bag most useful. I bought some good boxing gloves, a standing teardrop bag, and some basic instruction. Frustration, depression, or anger can turn to strength and even enjoyment as you learn to deliver a satisfying punch. Another option I've enjoyed involves finding a secluded ridge over a creek bed or other body of water. Haul some rocks of throwable size up to a high point and heave them, one at a time, into the water below, vocalizing loudly and gutturally to help you lift and shove each rock on its way.

Even though you may entertain the thought in your mind, these exercises are not about punching or hurling rocks at a person or adversary. You are moving energy with your whole body, enjoying your strength, and welcoming the feelings that accompany this exertion. You may be happily surprised by the insights that surface on the other side of such energetic practices. It is especially important to deliberately move energy vigorously if you tend toward depression.

On the other end of the continuum, partake in what soothes you—hot baths can be just the thing. Certain music can be nourishing. You might ask close friends for their musical suggestions.

Pay attention to what is needed at any particular time, and allow your body's needs to guide you.

Connecting with Nature

When you feel lost and don't know where to turn, you might head for the woods or a nearby park. The earth will ground you in her stability, solidity, and constancy. Weather permitting, bare feet on the earth helps with this connection. You may also feel the urge to place your cheek on a rock, or sink your torso into the bark of a tree. The earth is like a friend who has no judgment. You may feel like talking to her. Listen to how she responds. She may answer with a soft wind that soothes even the most intense grief or hysteria. Or through a creature that comes to you, or through a calmness that settles in your heart.

Walking in nature can be transformative. Set out with no outcome in mind other than noticing the colors, shapes, and sensations that catch your attention. This is a wonderful way for those who have trouble with formal meditation to empty their thoughts and simply *be*.

Gaining a "Higher" Perspective

It can be helpful to look at what is happening in your life from a much larger perspective. For many, an astrological perspective can shed light on how larger patterns might be affecting your endings—and your beginnings. It is important to engage a skilled astrologer, as many work by formula, and their assessments may miss the mark. (See Appendices: Further Resources, for a recommendation.)

Resources

Pema Chödrön. *When Things Fall Apart: Heart Advice for Difficult Times.* Boston: Shambhala Classics, 2000.

The practicality of her teachings has made Pema Chödrön one of the most beloved of contemporary American spiritual authors, among Buddhists and non-Buddhists alike. This collection of talks she gave between 1987 and 1994 is a treasury of wisdom for going on living when we are overcome by pain and difficulties.

Elisabeth Kübler-Ross. *On Death and Dying: What the Dying Have to Teach Doctors, Nurses, Clergy & Their Own Families.* New York: Scribner, 2014.

Dr. Kübler-Ross explores the five stages of death: denial and isolation, anger, bargaining, depression, and acceptance. Through sample interviews and conversations, she gives readers a better understanding of how imminent death affects the patient, the professionals who serve that patient, and the patient's family, to bring hope to all who are involved. As other significant losses can often follow this same pattern of response, recognizing these stages can be very reassuring.

Mark Nepo. *Seven Thousand Ways to Listen: Staying Close to What Is Sacred.* New York: Atria Books, 2012.

Mark Nepo affirms that listening is one of the most mysterious, luminous, and challenging art forms: "Whatever difficulty you face, there are time-tried ways you can listen your way through. Because listening is the doorway to everything that matters." With great personal candor and sensitivity, Nepo helps us find a creative—in fact, liberating—stance in the face of endings.

Thomas Riedelsheimer, director. *Rivers and Tides: Andy Goldsworthy Working with Time.* DVD. New York: Docurama Films, 2006.

Relaxing into Andrew Goldsworthy's cinematic portrayal of the great cycles of forming and dissolving in the natural world will likely give you a way of relating more easily to your own endings and beginnings. This documentary presents an enchanting, artistic view of nature, and a way to quiet your heart.

David Whyte. *Consolations: The Solace, Nourishment and Underlying Meaning of Everyday Words.* Langley, WA: Many Rivers Press, 2014.

David Whyte leads us into the interior healing spaces of the words that shape our passages. Beginning with *Alone* and closing with *Work*, each short chapter is a meditation on meaning and context, and an invitation to shift and broaden our perspectives on the inevitable vicissitudes of life: pain and joy, honesty and anger, confession and vulnerability, the experience of feeling besieged and the desire to run away from it all.

unsettled

making peace with "not doing"

exploring new things

lost

unsure of who I am

turned inward

questioning my real contribution

feeling useless and guilty

changing old habits

doing what brings joy

awkward socially

enjoying being alone

anxious about income

learning about trust and patience

finding a slower rhythm

3

The Dwelling Place of In-Between: Waves and Troughs

Trough

There is a trough in waves,
A low spot
Where horizon disappears
And only sky
And water
Are our company.

And there we lose our way
Unless
We rest, knowing the wave will bring us
To its crest again.

There we may drown
If we let fear
Hold us within its grip and shake us
Side to side,
And leave us flailing, torn, disoriented.

But if we rest there
In the trough,
Are silent,
Being with
The low part of the wave,
Keeping
Our energy and
Noticing the shape of things,

The flow,
Then time alone
Will bring us to another
Place
Where we can see
Horizon, see the land again,
Regain our sense
Of where
We are,
And where we need to swim.

JUDY BROWN

$\mathcal{T}$he time comes when our stay in the Dwelling Place of Endings itself comes to an end. Some chapter of our life is really over, acknowledged, and marked. Waves of nostalgia and doubt about our choices may yet wash up on our shores. Fundamentally, though, we are shifting our attention out of the past and into where we are now, the Dwelling Place of In-Between. In one of her workshops about coming to terms with death, Elisabeth Kübler-Ross ponders how we know when some part of our life is really over and we are ready for the next step: "As with the migrant birds, there is a voice within, if only we would listen to it, that tells us so certainly when to go forth into the unknown."

Entering the Dwelling Place of In-Between is entering the unknown. A whole new set of feelings and challenges presents itself. The threshold of this new phase of transition might be experienced as a great out-breath or sigh of relief. If you have been through an ending cycle that has been fraught with intense emotions, residual tensions may have lodged in your body. It may be time for a respite, so that the stress can gently unwind in whatever way works for you. Rest and recuperation are likely needed.

Lifting your eyes to scan new and unfamiliar terrain, you may feel disorientated, as if you've lost connection to who you are. If the ending was major or traumatic, a clear direction forward and a new sense of Self are likely hidden from view. The specter of "not knowing" raises its head, and uneasiness travels as its companion. We are asked to bravely and willingly stand in a void.

In 1854, Henry David Thoreau, the nineteenth-century American writer and philosopher, wrote this in his journal: "Most men [and women] are engaged in busyness the greater part of their lives, because the soul abhors a vacuum, and they have not discovered any continuous employment for man's nobler faculties."

Perhaps, though, the soul actually *craves* a vacuum, so that discovery of employment for our "nobler faculties" can be discovered. The "busyness" Thoreau refers to can be understood as dogged adherence to a path followed in a former era of your life. The new employment that rises out of that vacuum—the Dwelling Place of In-Between—is worthy of who you are becoming.

But in this unfamiliar place, in this time of not know-ing, we may ask ourselves, "How do I tune my ear to direction from inside me? How do I stave off the world's prescriptions for me? What do I do when it seems as if nothing is happening?"

Holding Space Open for the Unknown

In her teenage years in Britain, Florence Nightingale (1820–1910) spent long hours in her family's formal English garden, paying close attention through each season to the growing cycles of the plants. She recalled a pivotal moment in her life when she was seventeen years old, notebook in hand, studying the patterns of new sprouts in early spring. Suddenly, she was filled with a "presence" larger than herself and the distinct sensation of being filled with a life purpose. She described a *feeling* of destiny that spread through her, and her confusion about what that might look like in terms of actions and choices. Trusting the undefined yet definite sensation, she made a decision to remain open to whatever might be calling her. Angering her mother, Nightingale rejected marriage proposals and the path of motherhood, instead choosing to hone her interests in science and medical studies, still without knowing to what end. Over and over, she turned down options that did not feel right, courageously holding out for "the real thing."

In 1854, reports came back to Britain about the horrific conditions for the wounded in the Crimean War. Breaking the restrictive social code for young, affluent English women, Nightingale trained a team of volunteers, then traveled with them to the front lines to help. Her health studies became immediately relevant. The team found that, because of the army's official indifference, overworked medical staff was delivering poor care to the wounded soldiers. Medicines were in short supply, hygiene was neglected, and mass infections—many of them fatal—were common. Nightingale raised the necessary funds from her personal contacts in Britain to rebuild the camps, paying strict attention to hygiene and sanitary conditions, and was able to reduce the death rate from 42% to 2%. Tirelessly visiting soldiers all through the night by the light of her lamp, she became known as a "ministering angel."

Nightingale's determination and vision raised the work of nursing to a respectable profession. In 1860, she founded the world's first nursing school, in London, and eventually inspired the entire field of medicine with her scientific rigor and dedication. When, later in life, Nightingale's sister asked her how she had recognized her true path, she reflected, "I said no over and over, disappointing many people, remaining dedicated to my scientific interests like a covenant with God. Eventually the path rose up around me until I was walking in the direction I was meant to go."

Destiny has as many forms as there are people, and comprehending your path can be the work of a lifetime. How convenient it would be to have a simple formula that leads to *The Answer*. But as we stumble forward without such a formula, our social milieu rushes in to fill the space with time pressures and suggestions, just as the norms of upper-class England pushed Florence Nightingale toward a traditional female role as wife and mother. Without a framework within which to understand the value of the undefined interim season before us, we may capitulate to such outer dictates. Setting goals and jumping into strategic planning for the next chapter of our lives before feeling where we are meant to go can obscure what the Field of Possibility holds for us. But when we understand the need for an open-ended space of transition, we become intrigued with authentic possibilities that are waiting for us, and our sense of adventure quickens.

One of the graduates of our CIYO program was asked to teach, in an MBA program at Columbia University, a course designed to help students navigate their life choices following graduation. She introduced the idea of a period of time to allow for reflection and regrouping when, during their career, some aspect of their work might come to a close. One young man objected to this idea of a period of unstructured, exploratory transition: "If new beginnings don't butt right up against endings, you've got a case of bad planning."

Such a strategy might work—until the soul cries out for input regarding the way forward. Alternatively, there is a profound re-creative process that the Dwelling Place of In-Between invites us to enter. We need to be still enough for new possibilities to find us. We need to stay put in the unformed place for as long as it takes, trusting that the way will become clear. Can we deliberately hold that space open long enough to perceive what outer movement(s) might be congruent with the deeper aspirations we hold?

Without understanding the value of the Dwelling Place of In-Between, we might be inclined to *think* our way into a new phase of life. Sometimes, people are encouraged to do an exercise to create a vision of what they really want, then proceed to formulate an action plan. This approach, though, is still based on the assumption that we can create a desired future by exerting our mind and our will. Vision and planning are useful—but usually *after* a direction has risen into focus. I have coached many women who report that the new direction they implement on the heels of a significant ending simply gets no traction. Such inertia is often the result of holding on to outdated motivations and intensions that have previously driven their lives. Trusting that new possibilities lie ahead despite your inability to see them from the trough you are in, it is easier to relax in the void.

Diving into the Dwelling Place of In-Between

So what does one actually *do* while waiting for authentic guidance from within that will open the way to the next phase of life? Dwelling in this transitional zone can feel very risky. What if this drought lasts forever? What will happen if nothing happens? Some women make pilgrimages back to their family roots. Others spend time alone in nature. In her book *Wild: From Lost to Found on the Pacific Coast Trail*, Sheryl Strayed writes about a trek on the Pacific Crest Trail that shifted her out of the trauma of a divorce and her mother's death. Writing a memoir may help to honor your past. Perhaps going back to school, as did Gina when she was recovering from the IVF trials, can be a good way to explore and develop interests, even if your studies don't link to a specific next step. In Maaianne's case, learning to make soap and gathering medicinal plants near her village in Zimbabwe animated happy rhythmic movement in her body and heart, which led to her new life work of dance. Developing a musical inclination may open up your confidence by letting you know that it's okay to simply do what you love. Maybe, for some unknown reason, you've always wanted to learn Italian. We just never know what will come of the pursuits that attract us, or what we might learn along the way. Speaking with other women who've been through a similar passage may be comforting, and they may have suggestions about other ways to embrace an unfamiliar and disorienting period of transition.

Not long after my first marriage ended, I lost my moorings and felt completely uninspired by the work options before me. I began to suspect that this disconnection from both my work and my marriage were, at root, reflections of a more fundamental disconnection within myself. Looming large was a question: Who am I?

Hoping I might find the answer at a spiritual retreat, I signed up for a workshop in California. I was living in McLeod, Montana, and knew my beat-up pickup truck wouldn't survive the trip, so I went to the ride exchange center at Montana State University in Bozeman. Flipping through the postings, I noticed a "RIDERS WANTED" ad seeking passengers for a small plane headed to Anchorage. Alaska was nowhere on my radar screen, but for some reason the request caught my attention. I canceled my reservation at the retreat and commandeered my sister, Anita, to join me. A week after reading the notice, we were standing on the tarmac at the Bozeman airport with the pilot of a tiny prop plane. Seeing the size of the plane, and having researched the size of the mountains we had to cross, Anita and I got very nervous. We would soon learn that our concerns were entirely warranted.

The trip north took us over massive, snow-clad ranges to the headwaters of the Matanuska River, which eventually meets the sea at Anchorage. It was an exhilarating ride over pristine white glaciers for hours on end—until the final descent. The pilot located the Matanuska and began to follow its course. When the altimeter registered 2000 feet, we flew into a narrowing canyon with extremely steep granite walls.

Fog began to gather above us, eliminating the option of increasing altitude, if necessary. Because the pilot had no instrument rating and was restricted to visual flight, we needed to keep the river in view. The fog steadily descended, forcing us lower and lower, sandwiching us between the fog and the crashing glacial river below. There was only one way to go, and that was straight ahead.

We looked to the pilot for reassurance and saw streams of sweat pouring down his face. Though we had been raised Unitarians and had never prayed a day in our lives, Anita and I held hands and prayed. Just as the fog was dropping down onto the river, the short runway appeared on a narrow strip of land by the water. After we'd taxied to a stop, all three of us leapt out and literally kissed the ground.

Sometimes it's not till we throw ourselves to the winds that we encounter the invisible net of the Field of Possibility that has been there all along. In the Dwelling Place of In-Between we may be called to surrender to a flow of an unexpected journey. In our case, the only plan my sister and I had after arriving in Alaska was to eventually take a ferry back down to Seattle. We donned our backpacks and began figuring out what to do, following whatever beckoned. This was the first time in my adult life that I let go into a flow of events that I had not managed ahead of time.

The web of synchronicities and just-in-time support persisted. As the days rolled by, surprising options opened one by one. Generous people took us into their homes. A hair-raising encounter with a mama grizzly bear convinced us to abandon a hiking trip at the base of Denali. To pay for our continued adventure, we took jobs in a cannery and painted boat bottoms in a coastal harbor. We hitchhiked from airstrip to airstrip, catching rides with commuters who were flying to work in distant villages and sportsmen who were heading into the wild. Looking back, I feel as though life—or the Great Spirit, as I sometimes call it—had deliberately laid out this path to prove its own presence and trustworthiness. This was my first conscious encounter with what I have come to know as the Field of Possibility, and it has informed everything I now do in my life. It took an unstructured transition period following the end of my first marriage to feel the reality of life's support and guiding hand. Nervous about every step at first, I slowly learned to trust the unfolding of events. I could not have had a better spiritual retreat.

While that trip to Alaska taught me how to let go and trust, other women crossing into the Dwelling Place of In-Between have been offered different lessons. Many of us who have been through midlife hormonal changes know that the estrogen crash that commonly occurs in the late forties or early fifties is a rite of passage itself, through the unknown and into, ultimately, a new version of who we are.

Sarah led Sunday-morning movement sessions that were a highlight of my week. In a dance hall above a downtown art gallery, Sarah quieted the room by reciting poetry, then played two hours of music, inviting us to be moved by subtle impulses from within. Sometimes she chose lyrical melodies and sometimes wild African rhythms—all of them felt sacred to me. On Sunday mornings I'd say to my husband, "I'm going to Chance"—my melding of *church* and *dance*.

Over the years and many cups of tea, Sarah and I became good friends. She'd take me to her art studio to see her latest experimentation with new mediums, or read me chapters of the memoir she was writing. Her endless energy poured into her dance classes and her yoga instruction. I learned that Sarah was one of the best massage therapists in town, but she was booked so far in advance that I found it almost impossible to get an appointment with her.

Then, in her late forties, perimenopause hit Sarah in full, sweaty force. Her verve and ambition plummeted. Dedicated to natural healing, Sarah rejected hormone replacement therapy, even though the hormonal roller coaster made it impossible for her to meet the physical demands of her multiple jobs. Except for a pared-down massage practice to earn a minimal income, she suspended all work. She let go of any friendships that drained her vitality, and told her students she was on indefinite retreat. She gave herself permission to rest. Over our traditional tea, Sarah said the most difficult thing for her was not knowing where she was headed. She revealed that her parents had drummed into her that knowing exactly what you are doing *is security, is power, is what counts.* But no matter how hard she now pushed into the emptiness for some definition of what was to come, there was no answer.

A year into her "sabbatical," she told me:

> I am in between who I was and who I am becoming. My hormonal waves tell me that soon I will no longer have eggs. I am feeling sad about never having had children, feeling anxious about what the future will be like as an older woman. Jumbled all together is resistance to aging, spurts of curiosity, lots of caution, and moments of surrender.

Sarah found ways to navigate this Place of In-Between. When she felt overwhelmed, she blurted her jumble of grief and confusion to her patient husband, asking him to simply be with her rather than trying to help her figure out the future. When she felt capable, she danced her feelings alone in her dance studio, exploring the ins and outs of her breath and the new feel of her changing body. She walked by herself in the woods. She painted, without focusing on technique or a predetermined image. She listened for the next color or brushstroke that the painting asked for, satisfied with whatever showed up on her canvas.

In the murky waters of the Dwelling Place of In-Between, Sarah intuitively understood that it was most helpful for her to simply follow impulses that arose one at a time. When we are immersed in a creative process that invites us to yield to what is emerging in the moment, the mind stops its chatter, and all our faculties entrain in service to an inner directive. The very *feel* of an inner directive—that physical and emotional sense of rightness—is greatly reassuring in a period of not knowing. Faith in this wellspring begins to reshape our whole lives, its headwaters deep in the Field of Possibility. Indeed, this is what happened with Sarah.

After years In-Between, Sarah went back to school to consolidate her meditation and movement practice and published her memoir as a thesis. She founded a school that she calls Embody, in which men and women are invited into the depth and breadth of who they are through the way they carry themselves in stillness and in motion. Sarah walked out of her old life and the Dwelling Place of In-Between, into a renewed calling that reflects the stature and substance of a woman her age, in her fullness, gray hair now winding through her curly brown mane.

Feeling Your Way into the Future

Over the past twenty years, while supporting women who are in search of their path, I have learned many things. Right at the top of the list of "transition truths" is wisdom that says, "We find our way by heart." As hard as we may try to figure out our calling with our intellects, our minds are not designed to understand, on their own, "who we are." Learning to follow their hearts can be especially difficult for those who have found—especially at an early age—academic or professional success in the world.

Huijin (*WHEE-jun*) arrived at a CIYO course in eastern Canada, having flown 5,700 miles from Shanghai to get her life in order. I remember feeling pierced by the eyes of this young woman as she sat directly across from me. She seemed to be tracking every word I spoke with quiet scrutiny, testing for depth and understanding.

To me she felt tenderhearted and vulnerable, even as she retained absolute composure.

During that week, we learned that when she was a child, Huijin and her family had left China to start a new life in Canada. Working very hard to make it in this new world, there was absolutely no room for vulnerability or respite from survival tactics. She had waited years to be in the atmosphere of a grouping like this, where she could express her feelings and converse freely about her personal struggles and what she felt called to do in life.

Huijin explained to us how she was expected to continue a long family lineage of inspired leadership, purportedly going all the way back to the philosopher Confucius. She enrolled in college, then went on get her MBA, graduating with a 4.0 grade point average. "My nickname was 'The Energizer Bunny'," she said, "My friends and colleagues thought I was a bit scary with so much enthusiasm and drive running through me." Immediately after graduation, she was offered a position at McKinsey & Company, a major international firm. Even though each day there told her that she was misplaced, the standards of her family and culture made it impossible to relinquish the fast track to success—until it was impossible not to.

> One day I saw a painting of a ballerina bound up in straps. This is how I felt. Somehow, a perfectly good outer life had become untenable. I felt I had no choice but to tear the straps away.

Huijin left her two first loves: she ended her relationship with her first and only boyfriend and resigned from her first and only job.

> I was overwhelmed with emotions—sadness, loss, frustration, fear, and shame. I was unable to cope, and my friends and family were all very worried about me.

Huijin had been well trained by her parents and culture to suppress her feelings. When the pressure of dammed-up emotions became too great for her to hold back, they spilled out wildly, totally swamping her. Realizing that these were feelings that had been bottled up since childhood, Huijin bravely stepped outside of her cultural norms, sought out a counselor—and irrevocably entered the Dwelling Place of In-Between, where she would reside for five long years as she let go of the past and weathered her anxiety about not knowing exactly where she was going. But she was determined to find out who she was underneath her achievements. She told me, "Waiting for signs that showed me where to go, reflecting on my story, and, particularly, handling my intense emotions were all very difficult."

Between 2010 and 2011, Huijin did not have a full-time job and was not "productive," according to her culture's definition of the term. Yet she courageously continued to hold open the question: what work is purposeful for me? She withstood her fear that no answer would ever come. She entertained impatience, then deliberately let it go. She recognized the heavy judgment of those who didn't understand what she was doing, and let go of the shame that arose when she felt judged. She let go of the haunting questions that played in her mind: "Was I working hard enough to find the answer? Was I being responsible to my family, my potential, and myself? Was I throwing everything good in my life away? Was I just acting like an immature person?"

Gradually, as Huijin realized that an authentic new life could not be measured against her old standards, her panicky feelings began to subside. She learned the difference between outer composure resulting from the suppression of feelings and the ease that came when a person welcomes and expresses her feelings in a healthy way. Learning these things helped her to accept the inevitable ups and downs of life, and to ride her passing feelings without being overwhelmed by them. Huijin discovered that her newly receptive heart had sensitized her to the nuances of the Field of Possibility, which held the way into her future. Under her desire to break free of the straps that bound her, she began to actually *feel* what was waiting for her.

Over time, a particular theme kept surfacing: "The desire to help young people to develop as leaders wouldn't leave me alone." Huijin began to experiment, in Hong Kong and Singapore, with a program that she called Young Leaders for Tomorrow. Her program provided the balanced approach to leadership that she wished she herself had had along the way: a combination of the leadership skills, the mindset of service, and the self-awareness that had been missing for her. Looking back now from a healthy interweaving of heart and mind, Huijin wonders if she had needed the strong, disturbing experiences she went through to find her way.

> Given the tight wall I had built around my heart, it took a tsunami to knock me off-balance enough to consider who I wanted to be . . . and feel the answers that came back to me. I have learned to welcome feelings rather than be at their mercy.

From the Dwelling Place of In-Between, we *feel* our way into the future. *Our true life paths are perceived largely through the heart.* The main reason that I advocate for a deliberate slower pace in these interim times is because the heart perceives more slowly than the mind. We must slow down to engage its wisdom.

If we have trouble feeling, life is ingenious about finding ways to unlock our emotional realm, even if it means, as in Huijin's case, a breakdown. The indicators of Huijin's new path were the aliveness and excitement she felt when she imagined giving young people in China the means of having a life that is both successful and satisfying. Applying her organizational skills and strong mind, she made that dream real—ever since it was conceived in her heart, her program has been a labor of Huijin's love. Once we get a *felt sense* of a direction that fits our soul's calling, our brainpower can do the strategizing and oversee its implementation.

I find Huijin's essence in the words of Confucius: "Wherever you go, go with all your heart."

Juggling Responsibilities While Waiting and Listening

Huijin had saved enough money to afford a time-out following the significant endings in her life, and thus worked only part-time. Other women may not be able to afford such a long hiatus due to financial necessity or family needs. It can be a huge challenge to clear space for the Dwelling Place of In-Between while meeting other of life's non-negotiable demands.

With careful attention, however, it is possible to reframe the focus of your days to emphasize spaciousness. Perhaps, for a period of time, you can cut back on the level of emotional investment in your job, and allow yourself to be satisfied with 80% performance instead of 110%. Perhaps you could set up new boundaries around extended work hours. When in an intense transition cycle, it is wise to ask, "What level of responsibility for the demands on me is enough for now?" Then figure out how to reserve and protect the unscheduled time you need. You might find open time for journaling, meditating, or sitting with a cup of tea in the early morning, before the invasion of daily demands. This can be a blessing that changes the tenor of your entire day.

Some may have to wait years for the required spaciousness. This can be especially true for those in the "sandwich" years of raising children while being responsible for elderly parents. In Jahnna's case, shortly after her son was out on his own, the demands of her mother's increasing needs were compounded by an unexpected shift in her creative work.

Jahnna and her husband had been an unstoppable team, co-authoring over 130 children's books and lighting up the stage with their theatrical productions. Then, midway through their fruitful partnership, her husband was offered an exciting, well-paying job that did not include her. As he moved into this new job, Jahnna's creative field was thrown into chaos. At the same time, her aging mother's needs intensified. Feeling that her inspiration had dried up, Jahnna threw all of her attention into caring for her mom. But before long, full-time caretaking left her exhausted and depressed. How could she reconnect with her imagination and inspiration while still caring for her mother?

Jahnna came to me for consultation and insight, using the process I call the Symbols Way (See Appendices: The Symbols Way). I had asked her to collect symbols representing the internal and external factors at play at this point in her life, such as her feeling of alienation from her calling, her mother's health, and her writer's block. She arranged these symbols on a piece of fabric that represented the possibilities hidden beneath her stuckness, then looked at her externalized situation from four different vantage points. First, we looked at the situation through the lens of her feelings, giving her heart a voice. Her sadness about working alone and her fear of the future entered the picture. Then, from a higher altitude, we looked over the entire situation to learn how the various factors interacted—such as the decision to care for her mother because of assumptions she'd made about her mother's wishes. Third, Jahnna spoke honestly about the hard truths of her circumstances. She was born to write, and she would shrivel if she didn't. Finally, she stood tall, and embraced her path through the imagined eyes of a wise ancestor who was able to bless the entirety of her life, exactly as it had been and currently was—including her mother's aging and her husband's decision to discontinue their literary partnership.

Toward the end of this process, I asked Jahnna to rearrange her symbols into a pattern that, for now, felt right to her. As she experimented with different arrangements, she was struck with a brilliant idea that popped up, seemingly from out of nowhere. By the end of the session, Jahnna had seen a way to loosen the structure she had created, in which she was available to her mother all day, every day.

That evening, fearing she might appear to be unkind or ungrateful, Jahnna bravely introduced to her mother the possibility of other caretakers. Much to her surprise, her mother found the idea acceptable.

Jahnna then tested the idea that had unexpectedly entered her mind: to remodel a tiny shed in her backyard as a haven of peace and quiet, where she could reconnect with her muse. Her son and husband lost no time in helping her convert the shed into her private sanctuary. In that room of her own, Jahnna found the spaciousness she needed to listen, uninterrupted, to a fresh stream of imagination already bubbling deep down inside her. She was now partnering with a part of herself. Jahnna had found her way through a painful juggling act into new ways of fulfilling her responsibilities to her mother that were in balance with the time she now spent in her new writing studio, which in turn enabled her transition into writing solely under her own name.

Treasured Companions

When we are in the Dwelling Place of In-Between, a few sensitive friends can be extremely helpful in protecting this time of gestation. Their main job in this interlude, when there is little or nothing to show for all the waiting and listening, is to remind us of what we are actually doing. The people who show up to help us in this way may not be the ones we expect. They are, however, the blessed ones who are relaxed with not knowing, who can stay with us for as long as it takes. They likely have had conscious experience of this Dwelling Place themselves, and have come to trust it as a birthplace of new life. They allow us to take our time in the womb, like midwives waiting for the natural moment of birth. Their wise counsel and steady presence will help us suspend the urge to premature action, and keep us from losing faith in the transition already underway.

Once, when my husband and I were in the throes of despair triggered by a convergence of health problems, depletion from multiple moves, and diverging views, I reached out to a friend for some help:

> Things are tough here. I am not sure what is ending in the mix, but a lot is. My husband has lost thirty pounds that he doesn't have to lose. And I am severely stressed. A breaking point is not too far away. I can't feel life's support. I'm very tired. This is hard to write, as I feel like disappearing.

My friend and her husband offered to provide for us a nonjudgmental surround so that we could breathe, get some perspective, and find some ease at this juncture. They lived across the country, so we connected several times by speaker phone. They loved us both, and had no agenda for a particular resolution. They just offered time and presence, knowing that the overdue changes would, in time, become clear. As my husband and I relaxed in their surround, we were able to see for ourselves the changes that were needed.

If you do not have a friend, or friends, with this kind of skill and experience to support you in an interim phase, you may wish to find a perceptive counselor or life coach to help you endure the In-Between times, and to listen with you for subtle movement arising from within. Finding a superb listener who can feed back what she or he hears and refrain from advising you about your situation will allow you to develop your own ability to listen to your interior voice of guidance.

During times of personal change, a circle of mature women can be an invaluable support. I define *mature circle* as a community of women who have honed the fine art of *holding* one another, as opposed to trying to *fix* one another. This implies unconditional positive regard and the ability to see the essential truth of one another regardless of turbulent storylines. The members of such a circle trust that sustained, loving attention creates the conditions in which the next steps of each woman's evolution will become evident to her.

I was privileged to participate in such a circle for fourteen years. The greatest gift of that experience was our shared faith in a possibility as yet unseen, yet gestating like an unsprouted seed below the surface of the ground. For years, we put our arms around the endings, In-Between periods, and dawning potential in each of our lives, weathering together our seasons of change.

If you find yourself without face-to-face support in the darkness of In-Between times, you might reach out to an online support group. A source of support and inspiration can also be found in the work of writers who have found nuanced language to express the experience and wisdom of this In-Between time. The Irish poet John O'Donahue has been such a companion for me. I have often used the poems he penned to honor various rites of passage in his collection entitled *To Bless the Space Between Us*. In his poem "For the Interim Time," he reminds me that "it is difficult and slow to become new," and that faithful endurance in the In-Between interlude will lead to a new dawn.

You might listen to recordings of storytellers like Michael Meade and Clarissa Pinkola Estés. Or read real life accounts of women coming into their own, such *I Am Malala*, by a young woman who finds her calling after an attempt on her life. Beryl Markham's *West with the Night* is the story of the first woman to fly solo from England to North America, despite great odds. Perhaps it would be comforting to cuddle up before bedtime with a novel that you can take into dreamtime that describes a woman who finds her path, as does Dellarobia Turnbow, the lead character in Barbara Kingsolver's *Flight Behavior*.

Coming to Terms with Old Patterns

In what seems the interminable limbo of the Dwelling Place of In-Between, the cornerstones that were the foundations of our former lives are dismantled. Some part of our identity is dissolving. This pause and stepping back from business as usual is an opportunity to awaken parts of ourselves that might be underdeveloped but could directly relate to our new calling. These "blanks" in our upbringing can be the result of opportunities curtailed by cultural biases that result in a dearth of examples available to us in childhood.

For example, you may have grown up in a family of mathematicians and developed proficiency in your mental capacities, but perhaps have had little experience in accessing your feelings. Perhaps your new life demands more sensitive perception through your emotions and physical body. If, on the other hand, you have mostly navigated by an emotional compass, life may now ask you to cultivate a more dispassionate, conceptual perspective. Or, if you have charted a life course based on accommodating the needs of others or honoring their judgments at the expense of your own, you will likely be called to develop strong boundaries. As you become more self-referential, you'll learn to say "yes" or "no" more decisively.

It takes courage to look at what is in the way of a full, healthy expression aligned with our deepest callings. In our journeys, we are at once propelled forward by inherent potential and blocked by our childhood coping strategies. Children are ingenious about devising ways to survive when love, safety, and belonging are not provided unconditionally. Becoming conscious of these strategies and realizing that they are no longer necessary as an adult is part of the work of the Dwelling Place of In-Between. Letting go of these coping behaviors inevitably feels like a risk, as they have provided stability and some semblance of connection to loved ones, often for many years. But forgiving, reopening our hearts, taking risks, and regaining the power of choice are essential to developing and sustaining the new life that is emerging.

As we have seen in Sarah's and Huijin's stories, they had to learn how to risk not knowing, and existing for a time with no goal—something that, in their formative years, was unthinkable. In her In-Between phase, Zeynep had to come to terms with the need, ingrained in her in early childhood, to have everything under control. A strong first step in releasing this kind of programming in a new stage of your life is your awareness of its influence, and an understanding of where the pattern came from. The physicist David Bohm, a Nobel laureate, said, "Observed thought changes." By this he meant that when we become aware of the thoughts and assumptions that run our lives, they begin immediately to change and release their grip, and thus give us scope for new responses to the world that are healthy and appropriate now.

Through the many years of assisting women coming into their own, I have seen that it is nearly impossible to move freely into the future without first accepting everything that has happened to us in the past. Often, our personal history is not an easy pill to swallow, particularly when our backgrounds include traumatic events. But through the deep healing work we do in the Dwelling Place of In-Between we can carve out an inner place of acceptance and even gratitude for the totality of our lives. The gratitude is not for the trauma, but for who we have become because of the challenges we have faced. It is gratitude for the creative force of life that runs through us and for the miracle of simply being here. When we get our bearings in this new stance, we can look back and see the threads of meaning and purpose that have run through our journey during all the difficulties and struggles. These threads inform and lead us to the new beginnings that await us.

Holding Powerful Questions

The Dwelling Place of In-Between is the home of questions, not answers. Having the patience to abide without knowing is what opens us to connect with what the Field of Possibility holds for us. Rainer Maria Rilke, in his *Letters to a Young Poet*, writes:

> Have patience with everything unresolved in your heart and try to love the questions themselves as if they were locked rooms or books written in a very foreign language. Don't search for the answers, which could not be given to you now, because you would not be able to live them. And the point is to live everything. Live the questions now.

Some of the questions you might be living are: What is this impulse to mothering? What does success mean to me? What is this restlessness churning in me? This longing, what is it? What is my fear of change really about? Apart from my roles and family history, who am I? What can I trust? When do I feel most alive? Please, God, can you help me find my way?

You might check to see if there is a deeper level of inquiry beneath your immediate question. Journaling can be very useful in helping you find the deepest question in your heart. Be careful to avoid value-laden questions like "How can I become a good person?" These will lead to fitting into the world's expectations rather than uncovering your own path.

Honest, open-ended questions are powerful allies. What are your questions? Can you linger in them, noticing what a sincere question draws to you? Clues to your answers may come from a book that "falls off the shelf" at the bookstore, or from a dream, or in your early-morning spontaneous writing. The subconscious often holds valuable clues and finds ways to get these through to us.

Zigzagging through the Dwelling Place of In-Between

Movement out of the Dwelling Place of In-Between into a new beginning may not happen smoothly or all at once. This zigzagging backward and forward is common as we move around the Wheel of Change. Michele's story is a good example of moving ahead, then backtracking into the emptiness of transition, as yet another layer of identity peels away. It's a story of patience, faith, and many test runs.

Michele was at the apex of her career as a producer for Disney Theatrical, with such Broadway shows as *The Lion King*, *The Little Mermaid*, *Mary Poppins*, and *Peter and the Starcatcher* to her credit. Most people would have said she was living a dream life—she was a senior vice president with a substantial paycheck and respect in the theater industry. But Michele knew it was time to find a new direction. When she resigned, her colleagues were shaken, and secretly inspired by her self-determination and courage to leave the glory of such distinction in the theater world. Yearning to create something of her own, rather than supporting other people's dreams and projects as she had been doing, Michele signed up for a CIYO program.

Immediately after the course, Michele was offered a job by playwright and producer Eve Ensler, author of *The Vagina Monologues*. She was tempted to leap-frog over her longing to take a break and discover what her own project might be. But after long consideration of the invitation, Michele had to admit that the job offer didn't sit well in her body. It didn't feel right to jump from one fast-moving train onto another. What she really wanted was to follow the pull toward something different, yet still undefined. Michele declined Ensler's offer, as seductive as it was, and continued her journey into the unknown.

After decades of intensity in the Broadway theater culture, the first change needed for Michele's over-stimulated nervous system was to seriously slow down. She left her apartment in the city and moved full-time to her rural property in upstate New York. There, she felt like a nobody and suddenly lacked any sense of identity. Michele felt deeply vulnerable.

With the help of a sensitive coach and a therapist, Michele bravely confronted childhood patterns that had driven her life. As a young girl, she had consistently over-achieved to gain the approval and love she craved. But now she was exploring her innate value, without needing the praise that had come with high-profile success. Over the next twelve months, she grew familiar with the troughs in a period of withdrawal.

At the end of this year the cycle of change seemed to turn. In the expanse Michele had cleared inside herself, she realized how much she loved supporting the aspirations of young men and women by providing a roadmap to just the sort of transitions she was going through. Using her connections and experience in Broadway production, she began offering workshops for students about to graduate from the theater departments of universities in New York. In her classes, Michele drew on her love of storytelling, understanding how touching and inspiring the narrative framework can be. Then, in her words, she "crashed and burned." There were more changes in store.

Her mother's health was declining, and Michele fell into the grief of losing that anchor. In the midst of this ending, her romantic partnership of fifteen years broke apart. Michele's remaining stability was her home, but soon it became clear that she needed to downsize and move on. Her deep grief and sorrow over these losses stalled her momentum into a new line of work. With each of those endings she was thrown back into the In-Between void, and the actualization of her dreams was pushed further into the future. No matter how badly she wanted the long transition to be over, she had no choice but to stay with the process.

Michele's journey wasn't just a remodeling of her life, but a complete reconstruction of her identity. Each time she was thrown back into the Dwelling Place of In-Between, she did another round of painstaking inner work. Slowly, she built a solid inner home base that would carry her through life's inevitable highs and lows. She relaxed her tight grip on the drive and determination that had paid off earlier in her life, and began to experience a sense of wholeness she had never imagined. Then, using her own story as a centerpiece, she moved into position to open the door to this hard-won inner stance for others affected by the uncertainty of our times and caught up in the speed of life in the twenty-first century.

Looking back on her life, Michele now recognizes the significant role her last project at Disney played in initiating her transition. She told me:

> *Peter and the Starcatcher* was a tremendous gift—the characters, the themes, and the spirit of the play. It's all about dreaming and yearning, courage and taking risks, connection and love. And having faith. Molly, the young heroine in the play, says, "To have faith is to have wings."

Indeed, abiding patiently in the In-Between takes tremendous faith. Like Michele, eventually your wings will carry you to the work and expression that arise from your wholeness.

One day, after you have forged a new relationship with your deep Self, something will signal a shift and beckon you forward into a new era of your life. You will know it by how it *feels*: maybe a wave of unexpected lightness; maybe a surprising idea that captures you and will not go away; maybe a curiosity or new interest lighting up. You will recognize the rightness of this new direction by the "yes" you feel in your body. At this point, perhaps new opportunities arise and new people come into your life as fellow travelers. These connections signal timely movement out of the Dwelling Place of In-Between into the Dwelling Place of New Beginnings.

How do we know when to remain in the Dwelling Place of In-Between, and when to catch the wave of a new beginning? It is possible to overstay one's time in the interim place, getting comfortable in the time-out and ignoring nudges to follow the signs and possibilities that are arising. If you resist the opening that has presented itself, a window of initiation may close, and you may need to live through another cycle before the portal into your awaiting future reopens. You can be sure, though, that the aliveness that beckons now will reassert itself again, in due time.

Helpful Practices in the Dwelling Place of In-Between

Journaling

Journaling remains a useful practice, now as a practice that builds up a tolerance of, and even a healthy appetite for, the Dwelling Place of In-Between. Here it is useful to journal about the past and what led into the ending that you have recently experienced. Casting back to turning points in your life will help you discern recurring patterns and uncover the origins of limiting beliefs. These are what you are leaving behind in this phase. Moving them out of your body and head and onto the page is a strong means of separating from aspects of your past that no longer serve. Floods of insight and understanding may arise in you. Journaling will help you ride the waves and troughs that are inevitable in this phase of change. Notice what triggers your ups and downs. Anticipation of rising and falling moods, and the gift of sight that alternates with the inevitable blind spots in the Dwelling Place of In-Between, will help you maintain equanimity through the unknown.

Free-form journaling may help you touch your soul's yearning, which has, at last, the space in which to surface. The yearning itself is a pulling into a future that is yours.

Finding Your Spot on the Earth

If you feel shaken or are losing faith, go directly to the earth as suggested earlier, preferably with bare feet, and make tactile connection with the ground. Press your hands or your whole body into her. There you find solidity to ground your groundlessness.

During an extended stay in the Dwelling Place of In-Between, you may benefit from anchoring in a spot on the earth that is sacred to you. To begin, dedicate a few hours to wandering in an undeveloped area near your home, letting yourself be attracted to a particular place that calls to you. You may be drawn to the view, bugs in the grasses, or the color of the leaves. Over the next months or years, get to know this special plot of ground through regular visits.

If the weather is cold, you might take with you a thermos of hot tea and a blanket to wrap around you. The point is to make this a place of refuge and renewal. Take time there to "listen" with all your senses. Slow way down. What do you experience differently each time you go there, both up close around your feet, in the area around you, and on the horizon? What sounds do you hear? How do the leaves and mosses feel to your touch? What do you smell in the air? Do birds or animals visit you that may carry some sort of message? Watch the seasons steadily pass though this place, and let yourself internalize the natural cycles of change. You might record your experience through photos. Maybe you are inspired to assemble these images, along with words that come to you, and place them a personal diary dedicated to your relationship with your chosen spot.

Another way to attune with the universal ebb and flow of life is to regularly witness the moon's waxing and waning. If you live near the ocean, you might ponder the changing tides. Feeling the pulsations of change in nature will give you confidence in your own cycles of change.

Build an Altar

In a private place in your home or yard, create an altar. Build it slowly, carefully choosing items that evoke a sacred surround for your life. Note what supports you in the In-Between time, and find symbols for these comforting presences. The four elements—water, air, earth, and fire—may well be included in some way. Carefully place each in a clearing or on a ledge or table, honoring its beauty and unique qualities. Notice how the mandala of symbols wants to evolve over the months ahead, and shift placements of objects accordingly. When you need a resting place for your heart, visit your altar, light a candle, and sit quietly in the atmosphere of this sacred site.

Discover Timelessness

Enjoy discovering what brings you into an experience beyond space and time. You might sit down with a pile of old magazines, cut out words and photos that jump out at you, and paste them into a collage. Maybe you are drawn to painting or crafting, maybe to gardening or baking or dancing. Maybe your hands want to sink into clay. Perhaps it's metalwork or quilting or playing the harmonica. The main thing is to let yourself get lost in a flow. Don't aim for a saleable, sensible, or perfected product. Whatever you create will be a product of the same flow that will eventually scoop up your life. As you let yourself align with this creative energy, you will remember life's ever-present current and feel it carrying you into the future.

Shore Up Your Support

As described in the chapter on the Dwelling Place of Endings, deliberately contracting with a support team is important in the In-Between phase. If you do not have such support, please reread the section on page 57. Even one precious person who has, himself or herself, persevered through the Dwelling Place of In-Between will be a special companion for you.

Relevant Reading

Read books about "the dark night of the soul." Reading about others' journeys through the In-Between territory can be most reassuring. Steep yourself in the stories of saints, leaders, musicians, athletes, businesspeople, inventors, poets, and ordinary people whose greatness has been born of trials and darkness. The pattern of emergence will reassure your heart and mind.

Centering

If you do not already have a centering practice, the In-Between phase on the Wheel of Change is a good time to develop one. This practice might be a particular form of meditation. Sitting quietly and maintaining awareness of your breathing may call to you; a slow walking meditation can help focus a chatterbox mind. Walking through some form of a labyrinth can symbolically lead you inward, then outward into a new beginning. Perhaps a stretching regime, such as yoga, can provide an entry to a relaxed, open state. Perhaps participating in a Japanese Tea Ceremony may bring you into the quiet beauty of the present moment. It may take some experimentation to find what form of centering works best to lead you into stillness of mind and openness of heart. Don't be surprised if, over time, one form evolves into another. Avoid heavy discipline and rigid rules about the "right" way to meditate. Move at a pace that is natural for you, enjoying the experimentation and practice.

Resources

Lauren Artress. *The Sacred Path Companion: A Guide to Walking the Labyrinth to Heal and Transform.* New York: Riverhead Books, 2006.

Lauren Artress describes the art of walking a labyrinth, and outlines the purpose of the ritual and, in particular, its uses for healing and transformation. Walking a labyrinth can help orient you in the territory of not knowing, and bring you to the interior place from which an authentic life unfolds.

Christina Baldwin. *Storycatcher: Making Sense of Our Lives through the Power and Practice of Story.* Novato, CA: New World Library, 2005.

A true companion in the Dwelling Place of In-Between, Christina Baldwin helps us see how the stories we tell ourselves about our circumstances become the lives we lead. *Storycatcher* is filled with poignant stories that open the hearts of family, community, and self. What a perfect time in your life transition to reconsider the story of your life, and to learn to write and speak it in a new way. Baldwin teaches us to re-create a sacred common ground for each other's most intimate stories.

Paulo Coelho. *The Alchemist.* San Francisco: HarperOne, 2014.

The Alchemist is the tale of a young man's journey through the Dwelling Place of In-Between. Paulo Coelho tells the mystical story of Santiago, an Andalusian shepherd boy who yearns to travel in search of worldly treasure. His quest will lead him to riches far different from—and far more satisfying than—anything he ever imagined. Santiago's journey teaches us about the essential wisdom of listening to our hearts, recognizing opportunity, learning to read the omens strewn along life's path—and, most important, of following our dreams. Though about a young man, the story is perfect for women of all ages.

Phil Cousineau. *The Art of Pilgrimage: The Seeker's Guide to Making Travel Sacred.* San Francisco: Conari Press, 1998.

In the Dwelling Place of In-Between, many women are drawn to travel. *The Art of Pilgrimage* shows that every journey can be sacred, soulful, and transformative if it is undertaken with a desire for spiritual risk and renewal. Whether traveling to Mecca or Memphis, Stonehenge or Tokyo, one's journey becomes meaningful when one's heart and imagination are open to life's input.

Clarissa Pinkola Estés. *Women Who Run with the Wolves: Myths and Stories of the Wild Woman Archetype.* New York: Ballantine Books, 1995.

Within each of us lives a powerful force filled with good instincts, passionate creativity, and ageless knowing: the Wild Woman, who represents the instinctual nature of women. But she is an endangered species. Dr. Estés unfolds rich myths from many cultures with fairy tales and stories, many of the latter from her own family, to help us reconnect with the fierce, healthy, visionary attributes of this instinctual nature. Through her stories we retrieve, examine, love, and understand the Wild Woman, and hold her in our deep psyches as one who is both magic and medicine—and who may take our hand when we feel lost in the Place of In-Between.

Thomas Moore. *Dark Nights of the Soul: A Guide to Finding Your Way Through Life's Ordeals.* New York: Gotham, 2005.

Thomas Moore takes us into the dark tunnels that follow aging, illness, the loss of a loved one, the end of a relationship, a career disappointment, or just an ongoing sense of dissatisfaction with life. He honors these times of fragility as periods of incubation and positive opportunities to hear the soul's deepest needs, hidden in what I have called the Field of Possibility. *Dark Nights of the Soul* speaks to the healing power of melancholy, the sexual dark night, and temporary insanities. He links emotional struggles with spirituality and creativity, to draw out the gifts and beauty of the darkness.

Wayne Muller. *Sabbath: Finding Rest, Renewal, and Delight in our Busy Lives.* New York: Bantam, 1999.

This book is a gift to those who feel exhausted or burned out. Wayne Muller shows us how to create time for rest, delight, renewal, and a refuge for our souls. His stories, poems, and practices lead us to rest that refreshes our bodies and minds, restores our creativity, and reconnects us to our birthright of inner happiness.

hopeful

inspired

breathing fresh air

ideas sparking

connection

optimistic, excited

possibility pulsing

full

heartened

discerning Yeses and Nos

recalibrating back to center

learning to calm and ground

testing

open to surprises

zing!!

4

The Dwelling Place
of New Beginnings:
New Ground Appears

For a New Beginning

In out-of-the-way places of the heart,
Where your thoughts never think to wander,
This beginning has been quietly forming,
Waiting until you were ready to emerge.
For a long time it has watched your desire,
Feeling the emptiness growing inside you,
Noticing how you willed yourself on,
Still unable to leave what you had outgrown.
It watched you play with the seduction of safety
And the gray promises that sameness whispered,
Heard the waves of turmoil rise and relent,
Wondered would you always live like this.
Then the delight, when your courage kindled,
And out you stepped onto new ground,
Your eyes young again with energy and dream,
A path of plenitude opening before you.
Though your destination is not yet clear
You can trust the promise of this opening;
Unfurl yourself into the grace of beginning
That is one with your life's desire.
Awaken your spirit to adventure;
Hold nothing back, learn to find ease in risk;
Soon you will be home in a new rhythm,
For your soul senses the world that awaits you.

JOHN O'DONOHUE

*H*ere comes the sun. The light of a new dawn breaks on the horizon as you step across the threshold, into the Dwelling Place of New Beginnings. The early-morning light calls you out of the night as a benediction for inner work done well, and for now completed. You have let go into the emptiness following an ending. You have found the slower rhythms of the space between. You have un-hooked the grip of old habits and strategies that have kept you safe. You have cleared the space for your unfettered Self to blossom anew. Welcome!

With the breaking light come beams of promise. Dreams and inklings move toward you out of the periphery of your awareness. You may feel a heartening wave of possibility moving in your heart. You are not willfully reinventing yourself. Rather, you are paying attention to the quality and content of inspiration rising out of the Field of Possibility. Welcome the pleasure of forward movement, whether it is subtle or dramatic.

One graduate of the CIYO program used the image of the fiddlehead fern to describe her experience of the Dwelling Place of New Beginnings. A fiddlehead is the early stage of a fern frond, when it is still curled into a delicate spiral. This woman's slow unfolding felt to her like the unfurling of the frond. For others, new beginnings come as beckoning adventure, complete with wild ideas, physical intensity, and flashes of insight.

Welcome the surprises and indications that ask you to change your lifestyle, your location, your worldview, your relationships. Welcome the fear of change, and the courage to take the risks that change requires. Welcome aliveness.

New Interests and Talents Stirring

As aliveness stirs in dormant parts of your being, prepare to be surprised by your impulses and even outrageous ideas that may come to mind. Unexpected interests may draw your attention. Talents you never thought you possessed may awaken. Coincidences may not be coincidental at all.

For a new phase of your life to accommodate the new depth and evolution of your calling, it may be necessary to reclaim marginalized or unexpressed parts of yourself. To master your own finances in a new era of independence, maybe you need to overcome an aversion to accounting. Or, as a first-time entrepreneur, you may need to develop expertise in social media, even though you've seen yourself as technologically challenged. Perhaps, after decades of being one who helps others, you need to learn to ask for help. Some women who have spent a lifetime in the shadows may need to take a public stand. Or, conversely, life may ask you to step down from a leadership platform to explore an interior world.

In my early fifties, when I had at last passed through the worst of menopause, I knew I wouldn't return to the way I had previously lived. But what was awakening at this threshold? Quite to my amazement, I discovered a latent artistic talent. While I was on vacation at my husband's family ranch in Canada, my daughter-in-law asked if I wanted a lesson in oil painting. Me? Paint? My scientific parents had considered art to be a rather inferior hobby—my best attempts at art while growing up had been stick figures. Holly suggested I choose a photo of a painting that I loved and copy it. Dubiously, I agreed.

I chose one of my favorite Georgia O'Keeffe paintings of irises. Holly set up an easel and palette, gave me some basic instruction, and let me have at it. I was caught off guard by my delight in color and the pleasure of the textures of paints. I was shocked to find my painting beautiful to my eye. But surely, this was a one-off anomaly. I tried another painting. And then another. My self-image of being "artistically challenged" began to crumble as I discovered an inborn ability that has since become an integral part of my middle years. Equally surprising, later on, was the discovery that people enjoyed viewing my work in local galleries, and occasionally even bought a painting.

Discovery of new interests and talents may have multiple meanings. At first, as I was developing my new-found talent, I walked devotedly in O'Keeffe's footsteps, brushstroke by brushstroke, color choice by color choice. Following her so intimately, I began to notice something else happening—a deep inner connection with her began to unfold.

Georgia O'Keeffe exemplifies a woman moving brave-ly into the Dwelling Place of New Beginnings. In 1949, soon after the death of her husband, Alfred Stieglitz, she left her New York home and the prestige she had earned there. Following her heart, she pioneered a life in the stark high desert of northern New Mexico, a region that had been beckoning to her for twenty years. Single, independent, and strident in her passion for the land, she filled her canvases with images of sensual rock formations, sun-bleached skulls, and vast blue skies. O'Keeffe lived well into her late nineties, on fire with creativity even through her final years. Toward the end of her life she became blind, and took up the tactile work of sculpting, which she could do without the use of her eyes. O'Keeffe's life and artistic work has inspired many women, including me, to risk pursuing our inner calling despite challenges and fear of the unknown. For me, painting has turned out to be a blissful encounter with a process—and practice—of following inner impulses, risking releasing of predetermined images brushstroke after brushstroke, moment by moment. Often when I paint, I lose all sense of time.

Discovering my ability to paint, I found an inner aesthetic that now permeates all I do in my life. As I paint a particular object, I often find my attention focused on the space around it that defines the figure or form itself. I look at my home in a similar way—I am as interested in the spaces between the pieces of furniture as I am in the furniture itself. Or I look out the window and see the sky as outlined by the mountains. In this reversal of figure and ground, the in-between space has become what I am most drawn to. It seems that most meaningful things emerge out of this kind of perception. To me, it is a way of perceiving the Field of Possibility from which arise all things that resonate with the soul's longing. As a reader holds this book in her hands, I want her to *feel* the open, interior space from which it has emerged, as well as understand conceptually the natural order of change. I want her to connect with her own inner space, and get a feel for unfolding her life from this fertile field. I believe that when we create from this place, we bring to a fragmented world coherence, beauty, and hope—whether it be in the form of a meal, a painting, or a pathway into the future. This expresses my deepest calling at this time, and lies behind my dedication to fostering awareness of a universal creative process.

Following the Trail of What You Love

Following the trail of what we love may lead us to the activities that link us to the next phase of our lives. And, interestingly enough, following what we love often becomes a way of living that opens into a love for ourselves. At some point, a hidden passion may break into our consciousness, demanding our attention and directing us toward a new life.

Cigdem (*CHEE-dam*) was faculty for the CIYO program in Turkey for several years while maintaining a career in corporate leadership training. Her skill and professional demeanor gave her credibility on both fronts. But while Cigdem found satisfaction in her success, something inside her felt uneasy. Beneath her work, a deeper longing had lain dormant, and one day it was jolted awake in an unexpected moment of recognition. In the schoolyard to pick up her daughter from kindergarten, she noticed a four-year-old boy standing alone on the playground, crying. For some inexplicable reason, she found herself weeping with him. She remembers asking herself, "What is happening to me?"

Surprised and puzzled by her burst of deep feeling, Cigdem searched for other incidents in her life that had similarly opened her heart, and immediately recalled the birth of her first child. "When I held Derya in my arms for the first time, I could feel the blood running inside my body. I remember having an ecstatic experience of my own presence. Time dissolved." That same blissful state arose again when she took time off from work to be with her second baby, Kerem. In the intimacy of this time with her children, Cigdem had slowed down and savored the richness of each moment. "When I relax in the present time that children live in, I feel more like myself. I actually *feel* myself. I realized that, both times I had a baby, my connection with myself strengthened."

What did these insights reveal? As Cigdem pondered the question, it dawned on her that though she taught other women about self-respect and the benefits of following their unique callings, she actually didn't know exactly how to honor herself in this way. She had fulfilled the ideals and hopes that others had for her, but she could now see that she was most at ease and most connected to her heart when she was focusing on children.

Combining her leadership skills with her love of children, Cigdem changed her course. She was aware that parenting education in Turkey was sorely undeveloped, with traditional child-rearing practices that were unexamined for centuries. She dedicated herself to creating a program that would offer parents options for new attitudes and behaviors, which would ultimately help their children come into their own. This new beginning is bringing her life into closer alignment with a deeper calling.

Resetting Your Compass Bearing

The first four decades of our lives are usually about exploring the world and figuring out who we are—and, for many of us, who our partners are. Frieda was in her twenties when she enrolled in a CIYO course. She'd been working long hours as a waitress in a high-end bar in New York City as a way of supporting her passion for photography. But, exhausted by her intense work schedule, Frieda had little energy left for her art. She was in a decent relationship, but it, too, was draining; she devoted considerable time to supporting her partner's personal and professional development. He also wanted to have children, and was pressing Frieda into a marriage she wasn't sure she wanted. Frieda felt torn between her compulsion to fulfill his needs and the voice of doubt inside her about a relationship that felt as if it stood between her and her own calling. As she struggled to understand her tension, the roots of her dilemma slowly became evident.

When Frieda was a little girl, her older sister had a traumatic accident and had to relearn how to walk. Frieda had taken it on herself to be her sister's companion and protector. Later, when her younger sister was born, Frieda became her caretaker as well, never letting the baby out of her sight, and soothing her whenever she cried. When her parents divorced, Frieda, the middle child, tried to make everything okay on all fronts. She had spent a lifetime helping others, and now was desperate to help herself. Attending the CIYO course helped her legitimize her own needs and perceptions. Frieda was finally able to say no—and, finally, yes.

Choosing to make a new start, she moved on her own to a historic seaport on the coast of Maine. She bought herself a truck that reminded her of the earthy part of herself that had gotten lost along the way. Even after the move, it took a while for her to reach full clarity about the correctness of her decision to leave her relationship— but when she knew, *she knew*. In a coaching call several months after the CIYO program, she proudly told me, "I have good instincts." She said she was telling herself, "Good for you, Frieda, you did the right thing." When she felt solidly established in her new life, she decided to return to New York, get a less demanding job, and pri- oritize her photography. Now standing on solid interior ground, she magnetized a new relationship to her that supported a new direction without throwing her back into her old "helper" pattern. Frieda had paid attention to what called her, and, willing to do the work of exploring what was holding her back, she was able to recalibrate her direction early on in her life.

Many of us seek to rediscover ourselves around the half- century mark after having followed a particular trajectory for many years. Our definitions of success, achievement, and contribution often shift during these years. If we have tracked our movement on the Wheel of Change and seen how endings and fallow in-between periods can lead to new beginnings, our earned wisdom will more easily guide us through the reinvention of ourselves. If you have gone through transitions less consciously in the past, it's helpful to review, to the best of your ability, the way you have handled (or avoided) transitions in your adult life, so that you can see how you have here to fore approached the urge for change. Hindsight can help you purposefully negotiate change in fresh ways that allow you to more easily sense what is reaching toward you from the new life that is right around the corner.

Soon after turning fifty, Peri took a brave leap into that new life. At the time, she was a senior partner in a prominent consulting firm. Though she was satisfied with her work as project supervisor for several international contracts, the extensive travel that was required too often kept her away from her New Hampshire home, and was beginning to take a toll on her body. Peri missed her herb garden, and longed for a few relaxed hours in the old wooden rocking chair on her front porch, cup of tea in hand. As her inner and outer priorities began to exchange places, Peri realized that the lifestyle she had created, though rewarding in many ways, was obscuring the joy she knew was central to her Being.

This led her to an uncompromised search for an activity that would connect directly with her vital spirit. She seriously considered her attraction to gardening and herbology; both were delightful to her, but neither unlocked the outpouring of joy she knew was waiting to be set free. Then, at her company's annual Christmas party, Peri confirmed a direction that she had wondered about. Everyone else oohed and ahhed as they unwrapped the new iPads that the CEO had given them, but Peri's face fell. When he asked what was the matter, she spontaneously burst out, "But I wanted a horse!" Everyone laughed . . . but it was true.

Not long after, Peri began to visit equine rescue centers. Within a few months, she had rescued not one horse but two—having learned that horses, being herd animals, need company. On top of that, she took home a pregnant cat that had taken up residence at one of the boarding facilities. Though she couldn't foresee exactly where this path was leading, it was clear that she was shifting her lifestyle. Caring for her horses required that she negotiate a steep learning curve and make a daily commitment to her new family, as horses traditionally live for about thirty years. However, a childlike joy was entering her life—this new beginning kept her constantly on the edge between a belly laugh and "nerves" over her new responsibilities. As she mixed oats for her horses on crisp mornings in early winter, a soul satisfaction grew in her.

Since getting her horses, Peri reports having more energy and better discernment about what is worth doing in all aspects of her life. She now calibrates any choices she has to make with a "joy meter" that measures the new options against the happiness she feels in the paddock. Her relationships, being to being, with her feisty, 2,000-pound horses have opened a world of energetic connection that she believes is a gift to the world that is every bit as important as the leadership courses she taught.

Indeed, an authentic life, grounded in being true to ourselves, invariably ends up serving others as well as ourselves. As Cigdem followed her love for children into a study of parenting, she began to fill an educational void in her country. Zeynep's need for a break from her high-powered position in a global corporation was likely a factor that led her company to institute an official policy that allowed all employees a six-month sabbatical every five years. Also, it is common for women who begin anew at midlife to discover a sense of responsibility to and compassion for a global family, which reflect in new work that they initiate.

Couples Navigating New Beginnings Together

When a new beginning arises in your life, chances are that you're not the only one affected. Your new direction may change the status quo for your partner; then, your discovery process becomes something shared. Your partnership will have the best chance of evolving in a healthy way if both of you are honest and transparent about your feelings and thoughts. Courageous communication and mutual respect for one another's unfolding experiences are essential if the relationship is to honor the changing lives of both parties.

If we are attached to the familiar equilibrium of a relationship, we might override the vibrancy and potential in a pressing change we are called to make for ourselves. On the other hand, how do we respond to our partner's desire to initiate a new beginning that may not coincide with our own sense of direction? What if we are asked to follow our partner's path? If we want to sustain the relationship, how do we handle a new beginning that feels imposed on us?

I asked my friends Arlen and Andrée what it was like when this happened to them. Their lives were upended by the economic downturn in Canada in 2008. Each was faced with the challenge of finding a new livelihood. Arlen had been working in a housecleaning business with a friend and enjoying a full life. She was writing inspired poetry, and her love for music led to drumming for a flamenco troupe and local belly-dancing classes. She and Andrée valued their close-knit group of friends. Life for them had been simple and serene.

As the local economy collapsed, Andrée's earnings as a realtor rapidly diminished. She did whatever she could to pay the bills, including construction work and house painting. But her body, now in its sixth decade, wasn't up to the intense physical work. As their savings dwindled, her anxiety rose, along with a gnawing sense of failure. Reluctantly, Andrée admitted to herself that relocating might be the only solution. A few hours on the Internet led her to a town in Alberta where the real estate market was booming. When she made an exploratory trip to see what promise that town held, its dynamism and growth registered in her as a "yes." But what would that mean for Arlen, who was so happily settled in British Columbia?

Arlen had been married, and had two grown children when she met Andrée and knew that this was the relationship she had always wanted. Her sons accepted her relationship with a woman, but most of her family rejected her. With trepidation and excitement, Arlen drove from her home in eastern Canada to British Columbia to be with Andrée, all of her earthly belongings wedged into her car. Though it was a right move, the pain of the judgments and the fear of severing familiar connections took up residence in her cells and her memory. When Andrée advocated for the move to Alberta, Arlen felt traumatized by the prospect of another such move. The idea of starting over again at sixty-one was terrifying—she loved home and steadiness, whereas Andrée thrived on risk and adventure. Though she trusted Andrée's instincts, Arlen was paralyzed with anxiety. She knew that Andrée needed adventure, but Arlen needed to ponder, and as the pressure of her dilemma mounted, she found herself barely able to speak. How could they possibly honor their divergent needs and accommodate their couplehood in the new beginning that was called for?

To alleviate some of the pressure and give themselves time to think things through, they agreed that it would be a good idea for Andrée to move to the new town on her own for two months, to test the location and the job prospects. Andrée recalled that first step:

> I will always remember the day I went for my first bike ride in that new town. I was surrounded by fireweed, yarrow, and the scent of wild roses. I smiled at every person I passed on the trail. After a while, I sat down on a bench and started to weep: an odd mixture of ecstasy, relief, pain, and joy. After all these transitional years, I was in a new phase of life, a fresh and tangible birth. I was home.

Andrée was ready for the new beginning, *and* it was just as important to her that they take this step together. Photos of Andrée's new world arrived in Arlen's mailbox every day. The city was beautiful. It teemed with people from all over the world.

Arlen still found the *idea* of moving hard to face, but in spite of that, an excitement began to perk inside her. Carried by her love for Andrée, Arlen took the plunge, again packed her car to the gills, said goodbye to friends, and drove east to Alberta. "I arrived on a Tuesday, and two days later began a new line of work with someone Andrée had recently met. Much to my own surprise, a few months after the move, I, too, was home. Through Andrée's indomitable faith I have learned to trust the universe."

By respecting their differences and patiently exploring possibilities, Arlen and Andrée managed to enter their new beginning together. Remaining true to their individual perceptions and needs—and staying openhearted—they were able to support each other through the rough patches and adjustments they needed to make.

As Andrée and Arlen released their resistance to change, each in her own way, they opened themselves to a scenario they could hardly have dreamed of. For Arlen, that came with a subtle excitement that gradually grew in her, which is often how the Field of Possibility asserts its direction. The sure sign of arrival, at long last, in a new situation that truly fits is expressed so beautifully in Andrée's sentiment: "I am home."

New Beginnings: New Friends, New Associations

When you enter a new phase in your life, it is not unusual for your constellation of friendships to shift. Shedding an old identity may also mean shedding connections that sustained that identity. Unless you and your friends grow in parallel ways, or at least arrive at a new understanding of one another, some of them may move to the periphery of your life. Realizing that we are not in charge of these rearrangements may cause us considerable distress. We may want to dig in our heels, remain faithful, and keep our friendships as they have been—until we realize that the change has already happened. Though difficult, such changes in our web of friendships can be exciting confirmation of a new beginning.

If a friendship is based on shared work, common challenges, or overlapping purposes, it may fade away as the commonality dissolves. Though it can be awkward to overtly acknowledge the changes, it is helpful to speak of these dynamics when the occasion opens for a tender conversation in which you can, together, name the new reality. If there has been pain in the separating, forgiving yourself and the other can allow both of you to move into new configurations, or into an interim void in which you are more solitary. This kind of forgiving often requires deliberate and repeated returns to an attitude of acceptance and compassion, as your heart catches up with the knowledge that no one is to blame, and that the changes are part of the turning of life.

However, friendships that are rooted in a soul connection are inextricably entwined throughout the storylines of our lives, and can endure the intensities of change. I have a friend who has woven in and out of my life for thirty-five years, and at each intersection we have acknowledged our parallel tracks and appreciated that our connection is stronger than ever. She smiles at me and says, "Some people you just can't get rid of." This kind of friend follows us through every round on the Wheel of Change and is a treasure.

When we cross into a new chapter of life following a trauma or crisis, those who remain close to us are also changed. Our personal challenges can carry our intimate friends and partners through their own transformational passages, as parts of their identities are also burned away. In these cases the relationships become even stronger, fortified by deeply shared experience.

Other friends, however, may not be up to bearing the heat of close connection during a crisis and may drift away. My experience with cancer proved to be this kind of sorting process. Some long-term friendships simply did not expand to embrace my surgeries and the deep-seated changes in me that came with the necessity to face death. Though it is sometimes hard on the heart, I have learned to trust these shifts in proximity. Thankfully, I became close with other women, who now are integral to the new chapters of my life. Still, a poignant quality of grief accompanies the loss of close friendships.

Just as accepting greater distance between you and a friend may be necessary as you move into a new life, you may be required to separate from a community you have long identified with. This community may be a political affiliation, a social group, or a spiritual organization. As you grow into a new life, a chasm may open between the beliefs and values of that community and a different kind of knowing that is arising in you. If you are to remain aligned with your soul's journey, re-examining that association will be necessary, regardless of how uncomfortable this may be. Altering the quality of this connection may require courageous conversations with yourself and with others.

Elise was part of a close-knit spiritual group that taught selflessness within a framework of "world service." Honoring the tenets of this culture meant prioritizing the needs of the community over one's personal needs. For many years, Elise felt at home in this extended family, which satisfied her desire for belonging and association with a valuable pursuit.

However, by the time Elise was thirty-eight, her biological clock was ticking loudly, and Elise had not found a suitable partner within the organization. A voice inside her was growing louder, asking, "What about your own future? What about your desire to have children? And your longing to go back to school?" These aspirations ran contrary to the prescribed duties of the leadership role she played in the organization. And how could she disappoint the other leaders, whom she loved and admired?

Parting ways with the organization to follow the calling of her heart meant dissolving the sense of herself that had been defined by that context. This took strong resolve, and not a little courage—but faith in her inner guidance enabled her to walk away. Soon after, an unexpected relationship developed. She and her new partner founded a business that combined both of their skill sets, and children became a real possibility. They walked together into the Dwelling Place of New Beginnings.

Elise honored her emerging truth, even as it disturbed relationships that had previously given her a sense of importance and inclusion. Her story reassures us that, as soon as a particular context has been outgrown and released, the potential held in the Field of Possibility finds its way into the newly opened space and suggests a pathway that more accurately reflects the truth of our evolving experience of self.

One Good Step at a Time

Our new beginnings may require some experimenting and trial runs before we know which direction to move in. Going step by step, testing various possibilities, can give us a sense of how much energy *actually* lives in a proposed direction. Is the particular choice truly what you imagined it would be? Does it have a life of its own, or is it just a mind-made idea? Does your body quicken when you engage with this project? Do the practical means to carry it through fall easily into place?

"Sampling" a direction may mean renting before buying a home to see how a new locale really feels. Wise women walk into new relationships one step at a time with eyes wide open, testing to make sure that the partnership is a match that complements what the Field of Possibility holds in store for them, and is not merely fulfillment of a fantasy. It may mean first trying out a solution to a complex social problem on a small scale, and learning from what you discover. Feedback from others who are involved may help you refine this "prototype" as you move forward.

Master architect Christopher Alexander appeals to architects and city planners to use, in their design and building phases, a living process that moves forward in small increments, with opportunity at every point for feedback and correction. Building a town square that feels inviting is a good metaphor for creating a life direction that moves toward greater wholeness. Each is a generative process that at each step can be experientially tested for its life-giving qualities.

When I was part of a group that sought to design a sculpture garden at Genesis Farm in the rolling New Jersey hills, we were fortunate to work with Christopher Alexander and try his design process. Chris helped us identify the features of the meadow (trees, bush clusters, land mounds, animal habitats, vistas, etc.) that made it attractive to us. Then he asked us how we might enhance these features in our sculpture garden. We imagined fences that accentuated the comforting sense of being contained by the meadow, curving walkways that would reveal views of the surrounding mountains and cause us to slow down and take in the beauty, a small bridge to link open fields on one side of a stream to the magical hidden places on the other, while inviting a pause between them to enjoy the rippling sound of water moving over the rocks.

After thoroughly walking the land, we experimented on paper with the art installations and benches, choosing placements that invoked restfulness amid the groves and protective swales. Chris invited us to create physical mock-ups of these features to see if what we had imagined actually stirred the soul. We cordoned off areas with ropes where fences might go, set up chairs where wooden benches might be placed, laid a board across the creek where a bridge might be built. As we wandered through our construction, we could *feel* what it would be like to visit this garden. Based on the feedback of our real-time feelings on the site, we moved the fence over a foot, changed the location and shape of an entry gate, basked in the correct placement of a metal sculpture that we'd moved from an open field to a new home nestled among some shrubs. Chris's reflective, self-correcting process yielded a design for the garden that every one of us experienced as life-enhancing.

The same principles that serve creation of a living sanctuary can be applied to fashioning our own new beginnings. We can try out our new ideas to see how they actually work, then modify them incrementally.

Brianna had worked for decades in a state agency that was more about bureaucratic protocol than good works. When she finally resigned, she gave herself a year to relax and regroup. During this time she puttered in her garden, enjoying the feeling of dirt under her nails and the time in the open air. Her body recovered from a nine-hour-a-day desk job, and her vegetable garden responded eagerly to her attentions.

Brianna began to wonder if she could make a living selling produce in the rural setting where she lived. That second summer in her garden would become a trial run. She had never amended soil, built deer fences, designed an edible garden, built a chicken coop, or raised a flock of chicks. Her learning curve was steep. Did she really enjoy the hard work? Was farming just a reaction to her office job? Was it all a fantasy about joining the back-to-the-earth movement?

By mid-summer, Brianna was overrun with zucchinis and tomatoes, but her other crops were failing. She couldn't keep up with the watering, weeding, and harvesting. Realizing that she'd taken on a project beyond the means of one person, she asked friends to help in exchange for produce, which they were glad to do. Though Brianna's test run was proving exhausting, when she fell into bed each night by 8:30, she was happier than she'd been in years. Her soul satisfaction was fed by the challenges, and she felt thoroughly alive. She adjusted crop proportions, learned how to irrigate and how to more efficiently coordinate offers of help, and figured out how to sell her produce. Brianna's experiments showed her how to make the garden profitable the following year. She eagerly welcomed the winter months, when she and her friends could plan the garden based on what they were learning. Four years later, Brianna's experiment had grown into a small, thriving farm.

As we try out burgeoning ideas and possible options, we learn as much by noticing what does *not* resonate with us as by noticing what brings us alive. A sculptor frees a shape that is embedded in her stone by carefully removing what obscures that form. As she chips away what does *not* belong, the beauty hidden within the stone gradually comes into view. You may not find your "ultimate" new focus right away, and sometimes the process may feel like two steps forward and one step back. But eventually, as you continue to shed what no longer fits for you and pay close attention to what is life-giving, that which is distinctly yours will show itself as a valid direction.

Before that direction becomes apparent, in some cases, life may ask us to take a seeming detour that, in the end, makes our real destiny feasible. My decision to become a land developer (horrors!) was exactly that. In my early fifties, I had virtually no savings, having never seriously entertained "The Future." One day, it dawned on me that I would perhaps grow old, as most people do, and might need some reserves. At that time I was working for a non-profit organization that held great meaning for me but paid very little, and I could sense that a new project was waiting for me on the horizon, one that would require financial stability so that I could dedicate myself to a path that had little monetary return.

I racked my brain for an out-of-the-box project that would generate solid funds while working with people who shared a sense of adventure. My husband was up for the exploration. After months of searching, we connected with friends who were willing to invest in such a project. We noticed a tract of land that we could buy if we put in an offer before "real" developers grabbed it. We secured the property and began figuring out how to make this proposition real. We took on city and county roadblocks, calmed resistant neighbors, and blessed every tree that had to be moved to build a road and put in utilities. Four years later, we had developed lots for a green housing neighborhood that served our financial goals as well as our values. I was never destined to be a land developer, but it was a step that allowed me to continue working with that nonprofit and, eventually, to initiate my coursework with women in transition, which was right down the centerline of my calling.

Solid Ground for a New Beginning

If we have navigated our way well through the Dwelling Place of In-Between, we have learned to wisely let go of any tendency to barrel ahead as soon as options present themselves. We have learned to slow down enough to lis-

ten to our inner guidance. But when it comes time to ac-
tively engage opportunities that reflect an inner "yes," we
might be excited and seduced into re-engaging a former
pace, full speed ahead. Doing so risks losing sensitivity to
the Field of Possibility, which will continue to offer formative guidance. The Dwelling Place of New Beginnings
requires forward movement balanced with regular returns
to one's quiet center, which itself is the solid ground out
of which a fresh start can unfold in a healthy way. In that
place, we remember *who* it is who is setting off in this
new direction, and what is important to her. Without
this anchoring, we might dash down the wrong path of
opportunity. Or we might spread ourselves too thin as we
attempt to pursue several enticing paths at once.

Sometimes, establishing the solid ground for forward
movement depends on addressing something inside us
that still needs healing. Maria, a woman of multiple interests and talents, had no problem generating ideas for the
future. But when she had to prioritize one direction and
follow it, she was immobilized. Her home environment
reflected the same reluctance to let go of options. Maria
saved "stuff" in case she might need this or that one day;
the results were daunting overstuffed storage areas and a
mind cluttered with possibilities.

As Maria and I talked about this, she remembered her
early years when she was repeatedly punished by her parents for failing in attempts to be good at something. They
wanted her to shine in everything she did, and soundly
reprimanded her for what they judged to be substandard
behavior. These memories had translated into a fear of
taking decisive steps in any one direction—steps that

might lead to failure and her parents' disappointment. Recognizing the root cause of her stuckness, Maria was able to separate the risk of trying new things from the fear of punishment if she underperformed. As she worked through her fear, she was finally able to approach those daunting storage lockers. Cleaning out the first one was a victorious first step toward undertaking a single project to which she could happily dedicate herself.

In his poem "Start Close In," David Whyte urges us to take the first step—not the second or the third step, but the first: "the step you don't want to take." Jumping over that actual first step undermines all that follows. A close friend of mine kept this in mind when she was facilitating a dialogue with business executives about the mounting data confirming the reality of climate change. They wrestled with the implications for their companies, considering strategic responses to newly revealed facts about the serious threat to humans' ability to continue to live on the planet. My friend could see that, as overwhelming data spun through their minds, they were becoming paralyzed with confusion and fear. Deciding to interject the wisdom of the first step, she shared with them her own personal responses. She talked about how she and her husband lived in a house under 2,000 square feet, shared baths to save water, put solar panels on their roof, and heated with wood sustainably harvested from their surrounding oak forest. At the prospect of making personal lifestyle changes, the room fell silent. Then, gradually, tentatively, the business leaders began to reflect on their own situations, their resistance to "starting close in." This dialogue about real first steps established the ground for the exploration of corporate adaptation to the new reality.

It is good to remember that a new beginning doesn't necessarily mean throwing an old context away, but perhaps engaging it in a new way. Our past usually, in some way, contains the foundations for our future. As we saw with Zeynep when she returned to her former company on a new inner footing, a new beginning may mean approaching a familiar relationship or our jobs from a new stance, and adjusting our day-to-day behavior so that it is in alignment with this footing.

New Beginnings are likely filled with creative juice and high spirits. When we stay connected to our inner voice, timely options surface from the Field of Possibility. The field's instruction supports us in wielding the necessary "nos" that allow the winds of "yeses" to blow freshly through our being. We test and refine our direction, and in due course we are led to the Dwelling Place of Tending, where we unfold the deeper potential of our well-founded beginnings.

Helpful Practices in the Dwelling Place of New Beginnings

Journaling

Your journaling may now turn toward exploring the various scenarios and ideas percolating within you. You might try writing about these options, describing what each one might entail. It is important to explore what it *feels* like to occupy each of the various possibilities. After a couple of weeks, go back and reread what you have written; notice if certain themes reappear over and over. These are clues about future directions. If you lose your thread, your journal will hold it for you. Journaling is a safe place of investigation, of venturing into new scenarios, first in your imagination, with little risk.

You may choose to write about how you want to *be* in the world, as opposed to what you want to *do*. Try to articulate what brings you alive, what feeds your soul, what feels purposeful. If words don't easily express these qualities, try cutting out pictures from magazines that convey your sense of a life worth living, and paste them into your journal. Our culture supports the examination of *what* we do—but those who come into their own never lose track of *why* they do what they do. In your journaling, you may want to write about:

What: A possible direction

Why: The purpose of whatever direction you are considering

Who: Possible collaborators

How: Strategies to move ahead in a particular direction

Where: The setting that might best accommodate this new direction

Divination Tools

There are many divination tools that can be fun and instructive to play with at this point in your process. Some women use their favorite tarot cards. Some prefer runes, or the *I Ching*, and there are many other options. The value of such processes is that they can offer a glimpse into what seeming "chance" is sending your way, and an opportunity to notice whether what presents itself to you has the ring of truth. Pay attention to any recurring images or metaphors in these "oracles" that may echo the contents of your journaling.

Paying Attention to Context

This is a great time to read the headlines in the daily paper or to check in with news sources that you respect and trust. The focus of your life will not unfold independent of the trends and affairs of the world and community in which you live. Tune your perception to the arc of connection between inner guidance and outer needs.

Meditation

Again, any centering or meditative practice that calls to you will be very useful in the Dwelling Place of New Beginnings. Weighing options from the foundation of a still heart and a quiet mind will ensure that you are proceeding out of a true sense of Self, and in connection with the Field of Possibility. The process of discerning your next steps and their right timing is clearest and most reliable when you are centered.

Resources

Christopher Alexander. *The Nature of Order, Book Two: The Process of Creating Life—An Essay on the Art of Building and the Nature of the Universe.* Berkeley, CA: The Center for Environmental Structure, 2006.

I recommend this book only to those who crave an in-depth understanding of how life unfolds out of the invisible into forms that satisfy the soul. Though a slow and expensive read, it is one of the finest discussions of an organic, feeling-based process of creating that I have ever read. Alexander writes primarily for architects, but every paragraph can be read as instruction for those of us who are ardent architects of our own lives.

Herminia Ibarra. *Working Identity: Unconventional Strategies for Reinventing Your Career.* Boston: Harvard Business School Press, 2003.

Sometimes we long to make that leap into the unknown but hold back, still gripping, white-knuckled, the years of time and effort we've invested in our current profession. Herminia Ibarra presents a new model for reinventing careers that flies in the face of everything we've learned from "career experts." While common wisdom holds that we must first know what we want to do before we can act, Ibarra argues that this advice is backward. Knowing, she says, comes as the result of doing and experimenting. Career transition is not a straight path toward some predetermined identity, but a crooked journey during which we try on a host of "possible selves" that we might become.

Michael Meade. *The World Behind the World: Living at the Ends of Time.* Seattle: Green Fire Press, 2008.

Michael Meade weaves a tapestry of mythic tales and commentary that offers a "mythic inoculation" in times of great uncertainty. As nature is rattled and culture unravels, mythic imagination inspires and gives hope, for endings and beginnings are particularly mythic. When "the end" seems near, how we imagine the world becomes more important, and how we imagine humanity becomes most important of all. Meade helps us find a meaningful path through the times we live in as he situates our journeys in a larger context, evoking cross-generational wisdom.

maturing emotionally

finding balance

discerning priorities

accepting my path

satisfied with depth rather than breadth

recalibrating as needed

dependable and steady

taking my time

holding the long view

resisting comparison to others' lives

holding the tension of incompleteness

alternating hope and discouragement

tenacity

fulfillment

letting go of distractions

5

The Dwelling Place of Tending: Perseverance and Devotion

The miracle, or the power, that elevates the few is to be found in their industry, application and perseverance under the promptings of a brave determined spirit.

Mark Twain

The two most powerful warriors are patience and time.

Leo Tolstoy

The Tortoise never for a moment stopped, but went on with a slow but steady pace straight to the end of the course. The Hare, lying down by the wayside, fell fast asleep. At last waking up, and moving as fast as he could, he saw the Tortoise had reached the goal, and was comfortably dozing after her fatigue.

Aesop's Fables

In the Dwelling Place of New Beginnings your soul recognized a responsibility, calling, or creative compulsion and accepted it as its own. There you planted a strong seed; now it will grow roots. It will require your constancy in the Dwelling Place of Tending as you carry through to completion that which you have begun. Tending is the art and discipline of sustained attention. The rewards of this long-term stewardship are deep satisfaction and fulfillment.

Johann Wolfgang von Goethe is the likely author of the famous statement, "Whatever you can do or dream you can do, begin it. Boldness has genius, power, and magic in it. Begin it now." I would add at the end: *And if you expect it to bear fruit, tend it well over time, even when you don't feel like it.*

There are two kinds of tending represented in the Wheel of Change, each requiring a different span of time.

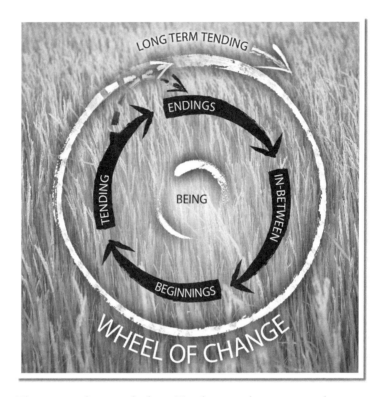

The arrow that symbolizes Tending in the inner circle represents shorter-term commitment to a particular project, as in the case of a student completing a term paper for a course she is taking. The longer-term commitment might be the years of focus required for her to earn a degree in her chosen area of study. Longer-term commitments are represented by the outer circle (joined to the inner circle by the dotted line). Taking on the problem of homelessness in your community, or creating a charter school that fits the present-day needs of local children, are examples of long-term contracts with yourself and others. The outer circle represents a steadfastness in the Dwelling Place of Tending that surrounds and interpenetrates other areas in your life that may be going through cycles of endings, in-between periods, and new beginnings. Often several threads of tending are happening simultaneously—as in the case of a woman caring for both a teenaged child and an aging parent. Or you may have multiple other projects running concurrently.

Such is the case for CIYO graduate Rebecca, who is in charge of product development for her family company, Badger Balm. Her position requires travel around the world and engages her visionary nature. At the same time, she has assumed leadership in a global movement that certifies "B Corporations": companies that have dedicated themselves to solving social and environmental problems using the power of business. Rebecca uses the policies of W.B. Badger Company as her platform to inspire entrepreneurs who seek to be not only the best *in* the world, but also the best *for* the world by ensuring the well-being of employees, committing to sustainable practices for the good of the planet, and maintaining a reasonable profit margin. For good measure, Rebecca also trains and performs as a fire dancer, dancing her passion for life in flaming hoop dances. Her allegiance to these concurrent interests braid different aspects of her being into a radically alive wholeness.

Rebecca's levels of commitment to each of these endeavors puts them all into the category of long-term tending. Whether our tending process is long or short, the same qualities of perseverance and dedication are needed until its completion delivers us into another ending.

Qualities That Sustain Long-Term Tending

In earlier chapters, we witnessed Arlen and Andrée tending their relationship through a challenging move and, in a new setting, into the next chapter of their lives. After initiating a new stance in her work and home life, we saw Zeynep's vigilance assert itself as she tended a delicate balance over time. Maaianne likewise changed the direction and quality of her life, then began the years of study it would take her to become a Movement Medicine practitioner, even as she continued to tend her family life. Other common domains of tending may include starting up your own business and seeing that through its growth phases, or sustaining a spiritual practice over time, even when your own resistance rebels against the discipline. Pledging to public service via ongoing support of a nonprofit organization or a political commitment are other examples of tending. Managing limitations such as low finances or chronic illness constitute another realm of tending that requires steadfast commitment for as long as those circumstances require. Staying invested in a job year after year is yet another act of tending. The stories told in this chapter speak of the resilience, persistence, and deep acceptance of the twists and turns of a journey over time that tending requires.

Women who have been caretakers for elderly parents know the fortitude and devotion needed for long-term tending. Significant amounts of money, time, and energy are likely required to walk this path. In the midst of this long and often arduous commitment, we have to give up many other options in our lives. It is important to maintain the thread of connection to our own creative unfolding over these years, though it can be challenging to walk the fine line between dedicated caretaking of a parent and tending to our own needs.

At the other end of the family spectrum, mothers worldwide are challenged with balancing their own needs with those of their families. However, it is true that the ferocious dedication required by parenting can also awaken a new commitment to ourselves. Sarah-Jane, a single mother, has faced the significant challenges of being the sole breadwinner while raising her daughter alone, and at the same time bringing her sensitive and determined spirit to bear in the world. When I asked Sarah-Jane to describe the devotion she feels for her daughter, her answer deepened my inquiry:

> My survival instincts were triggered by having a child, and I have no doubt that this saved my life. But it's important to note that my instincts saved *my* life, not my child's. Giving birth to Anna-Sophia, and then being responsible for her, strengthened my connection to my own blood-and-guts, embodied life force. I still feel this visceral connection, so much a part of the ferocity of my own contract with life. I never felt like a "devoted" mother, but I always felt true to the animal instinct that never allowed me to waver from fiery commitment and love—not just for my girl, but for my own determination to do the lifework that is mine.

In all cases, the Dwelling Place of Tending requires sustained focus, prioritization, and staying power. For example, the commitment to stay with the writing of this book had more impact on the overall ecology of my life than I could have imagined when I began. In my naïveté, I thought it would take me about nine months from start to finish. I misjudged by about two-and-a-half years, and had to recommit over and over as the actual scope of the project became clear. Along the way I went through three editors, each of whom altered my approach according to her or his advice—which was often contrary to the advice given by the previous editor. As I neared what I thought was the final draft, several people recommended that I consult yet another editor who had a strong reputation in the publishing jungle. She read my manuscript, told me that the book was timely and that my writing and platform for distribution were good—and that the structure of the book needed reworking. I was crestfallen by the prospect of the additional year of rewriting this would require.

After putting the manuscript aside for a couple months, I inched back toward it to start again, carefully testing whether or not I had the energy to commit to yet another round of tending this project. If my heart was still in it, I'd carry on. If not, I'd redirect my energy elsewhere. Knowing the paramount importance of the book for me, I regrouped and sat back down in front of the computer. As soon as I put fingers to keys, the text began to flow, providing me with the signal I was looking for. The calling to share what I have learned over the past decades of leading the CIYO program remained strong.

What I had initially thought would be a short-term tending cycle on the Wheel of Change turned into a long-term project that affected every aspect of my life. In that time my body rebelled against the many hours in front of the computer, and my husband and dog had to adjust their lifestyles to accommodate my absence; I cut back on other work and curtailed vacations. But in the end, by completing the book I had also completed a phase of my life, offered it to others, and was prepared to move on to the next chapter of my soul's work. Tending cycles requires perseverance and hard choices.

When we have fully stepped into a new project or endeavor, regardless of whether it is of short, long, or unknown duration, we honor our choice by carefully tending its needs and requirements. These projects provide very specific opportunities to face the self-defeating patterns that may keep us from coming truly into our own. As we deal with the discouragements and inner roadblocks that surface, we tend our own evolution and maturation.

We may never know the impact that some of the projects we see through to completion may have on others. I am reminded of the man who bought the house next to ours and proceeded to plant fifty redwood seedlings. He watered them  daily, until the taproots were deep enough to sink into the water table and thrive on their own. Although he will never see them mature into their awesome presence as adult trees, he was tending a project with a term that exceeded his own lifetime. Those who are dedicated to environmental sustainability know the gratification (and the obstacles) of such long-term tending as they work, often selflessly, for the generations to come.

Because women are physically equipped to give birth, many of us are innately drawn to bringing into form the potentialities that rise out of the Field of Possibility—as are many men. Moving beyond the magic that often accompanies the inception of a new endeavor, we find ourselves face to face with the realities of raising our actual or metaphorical child. Preparing the soil and planting seeds inevitably lead to tending that requires weeding, pruning, and storing the ripened produce. Starting a relationship inevitably leads to the hard work required in order to grow and deepen together in a shared life. The early stages of a business project may require vision, experimenting, and soliciting support from collaborators, while later stages may necessitate establishing policies and procedures, sophisticated accounting processes, and succession planning. Responsible tending inevitably asks us to continue thinking ahead. What will be needed next? This is especially important when we see our own part in the tending cycle come to a close as we pass a project on to others.

When Glennifer Gillespie, Beth Jandernoa, and I initiated the CIYO program, we had no idea how our off-spring would develop or what kind of care it might need over the years. As it turned out, we had birthed a program that would, for decades, meet the needs of women around the globe.

In the early years, we were occupied with wild and

thrilling innovations and program design. Almost twenty years later, CIYO's needs have changed. Now, spanning continents, it feels more like a movement than a program, with adaptations tailored to many different languages and cultures, and requiring broad organizational skills such as the establishment of global communication systems, facilitator training, quality control, more sophisticated financial management, and reinvention of our governmental framework. As the organization grew, Glennie and Beth realized that they were less drawn to the tending requirements of CIYO's more mature stage of development, and shifted into elder roles as members of our nonprofit's Board of Directors. From this position they could periodically offer input with a light touch while remaining guardians of the vision and premises that make CIYO programs unique.

Two other colleagues, who thrive on "thinking big" and enjoy grappling with systems and structures, stepped up to assume global leadership roles along with me. Dorian Baroni, with Italian and American roots, has considerable experience in helping global companies diversify and grow. Isabelle Pujol, from Belgium, owns a company that specializes in helping corporations address needs for diversity and inclusion in the multicultural world we now live in. Their business experience and interest in supporting emerging leaders are good fits with the cycle of tending that CIYO currently requires.

In most major endeavors, those who sustain a project are different from those who initiated it. As you consider your own role in the tending cycle, you might ask yourself if you are an initiator or a long-term tender—or both. Let your answer guide your choices.

Tending the Thread of Your Calling

When you cast back over your life, you may recognize certain themes that have captured your attention again and again. This continuous thread of interest is likely an expression of your essential nature and, as such, relates to your life calling.

Early in our lives, it may be hard for us to discern this thread, though it manifests repeatedly in many guises. The way I see it, the energy of the unique Being that we each are is, all along, influencing those themes on our path. As our self-reflecting becomes more astute, the pattern of this energy becomes clearer, and we hopefully become more adept at listening to its implications. Some of us might call this pattern our mission statement; others might refer to it as our destiny line. Once we are able to name the thread, we can purposefully use it to guide us through choice points that we face along the way.

Sahni was destined to be a healer, though she was unaware of this calling as she grew up in Australia. As a child, she had faced health challenges in a bout with polio. She recovered, though her body carried some residual weaknesses. She went on with her life and eventually went to college, where she followed an interest in anthropology. After she graduated, her studies inspired a trip to Africa. There, in the midst of a Saharan drought, she witnessed widespread starvation and malnourishment. The shock of it awoke her instincts for healing. In her telling of this story, I could almost feel her Being invisibly guiding her into the midst of that Saharan crisis. Because of what Sahni had witnessed, she made a decision to go back to school to earn a master's degree in nutrition, then worked as a nutritionist for several years. During that time she came to see how disconnected people are from their bodies. That motivated her to return to school again, this time to become a body worker and, eventually, to co-direct a massage school, teaching others how to heal through touch and various energetic modalities.

Her fundamental calling to heal whispered its essence to her and guided her way for years before she could explicitly name it. As is the case for many practitioners, her own health issues propelled her into a search for what healing entails on all levels. Her childhood experience with polio, and, in later life, challenges with blinding eye disease, informed that call. Sahni continued her search for a form of healing work that fit her clarified call. She trained as a psychotherapist, and gave twenty-five years to that profession.

In her late fifties, Sahni moved to the United States with her American husband, leaving behind her beloved, wild Australian earth, along with familiar work, friends, pets, and family. But she did not lose the thread that had been woven through her life. "What am I passionate about, and what does healing mean to me now?" she asked herself. This time, her call to heal broadened and deepened to encompass our compromised earth. She embarked on a serious study of the medicinal properties of plants, blending Eastern and Western knowledge of herbs to restore human interdependence with the natural world, for the healing of both.

Debra Silverman, on the other hand, recognized the thread of her calling while still a child. Young Debra became determined to figure out why her father never talked, why her mother threw things, and why her brother was an addict. And she wanted to make peace with her own quirkiness, too. By the time she was ready for college, the best context she could find to pursue this search was the study of psychology. She went on to graduate school, where she was certified as a therapist. But Debra was not willing to box in the parameters of her quest. "I'll do anything to understand what makes someone tick," she says. That passion led her beyond traditional psychology.

When Debra first encountered astrology, she was skeptical. But deeper study convinced her that she had found a missing piece that would help her understand human nature. She studied, tested, and experimented, first offering readings to her therapy clients, then responding to the growing number of referrals she was receiving for this work. As she might have predicted, at the astrological turning point that occurs at or near age 28, everything kicked into gear. She was given her own radio show, and the requests for readings soared. She was scheduling eight private readings a day. "Once I really sense who a person is at their core, I give them full permission to turn up the volume, and to help them fall in love with themselves." Following the thread of her calling had led Debra to earning her livelihood by helping many others find their unique threads.

In hindsight, Debra describes this intense application of her passion as a "spiritual practice." She says the call was so deep that she would have done this work for free— and often did, when no payment was possible.

By the time Debra reached a second major astrological life passage, one that occurs between ages 58 and 60, she was ready for another leap. At this turning point, she says, "We get to decide if we are going to get older or younger. Either people get back to their real rhythm, their passion, and retrieve lost aspects of themselves—or they begin bowing out." For Debra, this meant turning up the volume on her lifework. She finished a book, developed a strong Web presence, rebranded her offerings, and started teaching via teleconferences along with delivering many keynote addresses. Debra had recognized her calling early on and had never let go of her thread, tending it carefully through every stage of her life.

Is there something you have been repeatedly called to *do* or *be*? Is there a recurring issue or question you feel called to resolve, for yourself or in service to society? Is there an invention or exploration that has continually commanded your attention? How have you followed this thread over the years? If these questions evoke an answer, how can you guard, amplify, and tend the emergence of that thread?

Tending Your Calling in the Midst of Limitation

How do we tend our calling when we feel thwarted by limitation? The necessities of survival can preclude the luxury of doing what we want to do, when we want to do it. Following the provocations of the Field of Possibility may seem impossible, at least for the time being. If chronic illness consumes your journey, it may be necessary to prioritize care for your body. Or perhaps income streams dry up and you need to take whatever work you can get to pay the bills. Practicality reigns as we are required to tend to our immediate needs, sometimes for long periods of time, and it may seem that we have lost the thread of our calling altogether.

Ellen, a professor at a university in Tennessee, loved inspiring young people to be their brightest and best selves. But at the height of her career, she contracted a rare kidney disease and had to resign. After two years of an all-encompassing regime of treatment and frequent hospitalization, she slowly began to stabilize, though her new definition of normal life included lower energy levels and regular dialysis. Still, Ellen now felt well enough to turn her attention back to the work she loved—but how? Even the thought of resuming teaching at her university was exhausting, but she didn't yet feel ready to let go of that calling altogether. She held the question open.

Seemingly out of the blue, Ellen was contacted by Dialogue House Associates, home of a writing program that fosters self-development through workshops in the Progoff Intensive Journal Program. She had studied at their institute many years before, and the director had remembered her. He wanted to ask if she might take the position of Director of Advanced Studies, using an online teaching format. Here was a perfect solution: Ellen could both tend to her health needs and pursue her career, in right balance. She was delighted. Her deep calling to inspire young people is now being fulfilled in ways she could not have imagined. Her tenacious hold on the thread, while relaxing her sense of *how* her calling might manifest, had kept a clear channel open into the Field of Possibility. Those who now train under her guidance are deeply touched by her mastery of the content *and* the person she has become.

I have observed that some of the finest qualities of character and the most significant contributions people make are forged under the pressure of constraint. An unavoidable detour away from your calling can prove to be the very experience that draws forth that stellar quality of character that blesses the world, and is itself at the heart of your contribution in this lifetime.

As we have seen, Ellen's circumstances required great patience and surrender to necessity. Sometimes, our deep aspirations need to be moved to the back burner for an indefinite period of time—perhaps even decades—as we tend to other realities in our lives. I am convinced, though, that we can count on life's ingenuity to create an outlet for our gifts, even in circumstances of limitation. We may have to let go, but we should never, ever give up on our deepest aspiration or calling.

In her early twenties, Sandra had jettisoned her job (with benefits) in a corporate office environment that was filled with jaded employees. She had no idea of what she might want to do instead, but financial security was not her top priority. She waited tables, drove a school bus, worked on a garlic farm in the San Juan Islands off the coast of Washington, and packed fish in the tundra of Alaska. The money she made supported simple living and rich experience, which eventually revealed to her that what she most loved was crafting beautiful things. With the help of a friend, Sandra started a business making handcrafted futons. Amazingly, her company grew from a basement endeavor to a full-fledged business and manufacturing facility with two retail stores, as buyers recognized and valued her aesthetic.

In the intervening fifteen years, Sandra had entered a personal relationship and work partnership with a popular spiritual teacher. Her job had now become running his non-profit organization and creating peaceful, gorgeous retreat environments for him. Because she had invested the substantial income from her business in mutual funds, she no longer had to worry about income, and could put extra time into the crafting that she loved. Sandra opened a glass studio, where she made delicate beads and fine jewelry. A number of times she pondered getting some training or education to further her own career, but was led to believe that she "was covered," and thought that meant for life.

Then, in heartbreaking ways, their engagement ended. In the midst of her deep grief, a letter arrived stating that the bulk of her savings had been lost in a Ponzi scheme. She was left with subsistence funding.

Now sixty-two, Sandra was faced with the reality of aging. She used her scant savings to enroll in massage school. Her love for beauty now centered on her appreciation for the essential beauty of the human form and the people she served. Her practice grew slowly; to pay the bills, she trimmed back her already simple lifestyle. At this point, she was still able to create jewelry in her glass studio.

When Sandra's health-insurance premiums rose dramatically before she was eligible for Medicare, she had to drop her policy. She had never imagined herself being so vulnerable, facing the task of solo survival in her sixties. With no time or residual energy to pursue her art, she put her glass forge into storage. Because any health problems now meant cash out of her pocket, she augmented her massage practice by cooking for elderly people in the community. Yet despite these challenges and the fear of the future that she often felt, Sandra did not abandon her call to beauty. She told me, in no uncertain terms, "I refuse to let fear rob me of the beauty of this world, even in the complexities and challenges I face."

When I walk into Sandra's small home, I am enveloped by thriving plants that she has grown from friends' cuttings, and enchanted by statues hiding among the branches. My senses revel in the rich textures of hanging fabrics and the magic of the rattles she has carved from gourds. Her massage room is a sanctuary of healing color, gentle sounds, and carefully chosen artifacts from nature. The elderly for whom she cooks are fed not only by the food she prepares, but equally by the artistic way she presents it. Though she works hard to pay her monthly bills and her glass studio remains dormant, Sandra's calling is in full flower through everything she does. Once she had defined the thread of her calling as the creation of beauty, she found ways to tend it by infusing everything she does with this quality, while tending survival needs. Her happiness and satisfaction are testimony to the power of the creative spirit to find ways to express itself, despite challenges and limitations.

Balancing Commitment and Adaptation

The capacity for long-term stewardship is a mark of spiritual maturity and points toward ultimate fulfillment. A cycle of tending may carry an endeavor through to fruition and celebration of its completion. What happens, though, when a responsibility, project, or idea that you're tending is simply not working out? It is important to distinguish between long-term commitment and rigid loyalty when factors that once pointed to the merits of lengthy dedication change. Can we recognize when it's time to let go of something we've long and carefully tended? When circumstances change, can we let go of a goal we have set?

We may set a goal to have half a million dollars in our bank account to ensure that we feel secure for the rest of our life, even if it means working beyond what the mind and body can bear. We may decide that it is our role and duty to stick with an organization we founded, even if we discover that we lack the skills its further evolution now calls for. We may commit ourselves to a particular career we have prepared for, even if it becomes exhausting and is pulling us apart. While wise commitment and lofty goals carry us through the inevitable ups and downs of any commitment, rigidly holding on to a vowed intention may override indications that a course correction is being called for. Circumstances change; sometimes, it is wise to change with them.

For twenty years Anita derived great satisfaction from her job with a school district in Massachusetts. As a self-taught expert in technology, she helped teachers and administrators climb the steep learning curves they faced in dealing with ever-changing technologies. Her plan was to work in this job, retire at 65, then use her full pension to support the next phase of her life.

But her circumstances changed. Funding was trimmed in the schools, and Anita was asked to take on more responsibilities than were humanly possible. Each night she went home, scarcely able to do more than walk her dog, down a beer, and fall into bed. All efforts she made to alter the scope of her job failed. If she were to stay sane, it was clear that retiring ahead of schedule would be necessary.

Anita let go of the work that had given her meaning and a decent livelihood, accepted a lesser pension, and courageously jumped into the void. It took many months to unwind the stress and get the incessant buzz of the technology out of her body. She began the work of getting back in shape and making long-needed house repairs. Slowly, she began to explore who she was at this stage of her life, discovering possibilities she would never have found had she stuck to her original plan.

Fixated on a goal, we may override an inner voice that cries to live at a different pace, or has a different definition of "enough." If subtle indicators are disregarded, life may resort to a stronger message to derail us from a fixed path. The correction may come through complications such as the onset of an autoimmune disease, a nervous breakdown, or an accident. Life's intervention brought June not only a new direction but a new way of living.

June was a highly skilled engineer and researcher. Straightforward, independent, and practical, she knew how to set a goal and get things done. She ran her life with a tight focus on logic and accomplishment until, one day, she was literally stopped in her tracks. Shortly after a near-fatal car crash, she arrived at a CIYO course. Sparse with words and emotionally reserved, June was at first a bit of an enigma in the group—until she told us the story that had led to her enrollment in the course. On the second day of the program, one of the younger participants, Shawna, had broken into tears as she described the pain she felt at the lack of partnership in her life. In the midst of Shawna's emotional outburst, June broke in. Very slowly and authoritatively, she stated, "Everything is going to be okay." Then, again: "Everything is going to be okay." As the room went quiet, she took a long breath. Surprised at the strength and tone of June's comment, everyone's attention turned in her direction, and June asked permission to tell her own story.

June had come to the program shortly after that car crash, in which she'd been knocked unconscious. "I awoke briefly at the scene to know that 'others' were involved. That others ran a stop sign. That others included a baby. Then I was out again." She woke again in the ambulance, her mind racing as she frantically tried to remember what had happened. Overcome by fear, confusion, grief, and anxiety, she tried to get things ordered in her mind, but to no avail. Finally, she let go.

What happened next changed June's life. A great light flooded her vision. She distinctly heard a woman's powerful and loving voice speak directly to her: "Everything is okay. Everyone is okay. Let go. Just breathe. Know that everything is okay."

Strange as it was to her, the presence of that voice was irrefutable. June surrendered to the command and breathed.

And I knew. I *knew* that she was right. I felt calm, pain-free, worry-free, even euphoric. No words can describe the state I experienced. The feeling lasted a few hours, through all the tests, the questions, the prodding and poking at the hospital. During those hours, I did a lot of thinking and reflecting. I realized that it was time to change my approach to life.

The intensity of the voice began to fade after a few days, but the impact of the experience lived on. June signed up for CIYO even though that meant entering unfamiliar territory. I believe that the tenor and wisdom with which June intervened in Shawna's distress, saying, "Everything will be okay," was not unlike the authority of the voice that had spoken to her. Following her interjection into Shawna's story, June bloomed as a light in the group; her charm and humor graced us all. The reassurance that June had implanted in Shawna was evident for the remainder of our time together in the way she relaxed into trusting the unique unfolding of her life.

Following the accident—her course correction—June began to tend her life in a new way. She let go of her frenetic goal-orientation, and no longer rushed from one thing to the next. As she learned to slow down and listen to what called to her, the world became for her a brighter, more inviting place.

Crises that interrupt long-term plans, and that may feel like inconveniences or roadblocks, can often be rites of passage that invite re-evaluation of our priorities and frames of reference. They change our understanding of what is worth tending. Once we let go of thinking we simply need to "get over the inconveniences" and return to our former ways, we may notice that the course correction has been life's ingenious way of bringing us closer to our deeper calling.

The art of tending is an ongoing balancing act between commitment and accommodation of the needs of others. Being creatures who care about people, and who are at the same time charged with bringing forth a unique expression from within, we are constantly melding the two forces. Marriages that maintain their vitality over decades are a good model of this sensitive balancing act. Some couples annually refresh their commitment to one another, redefining precisely what they are committed to as their lives and their consciousnesses change. A wedding anniversary becomes an opportunity to review the pleasures and challenges of the last year and redefine their promise for the next twelve months. Tending a *living* commitment to each other ensures that their marriages are not simply loyalties to staying together. Loyalty at a deeper level may mean promising to support one another's unfolding aspirations, or committing to share feelings and really listen to one another's inner experience. It may be a vow to accommodate diverse interests even if that means time apart, or to express delicate matters that relate to changing sexual desires. Regular, honest reflection ensures that they are tending an evolving journey together, not just an image of what marriage looks like and a legal contract. The challenge, of course, in this quality of relationship is that it will hardly ever conform to what you imagine the marriage to be.

The women in this chapter have been tried and transformed in the slow-burning fires of the Dwelling Place of Tending. Wise tending develops a gravitas—a spiritual weightiness—and an awareness that the deeper gifts of character are as important as the contributions we make through our visible work. In the next and final chapter we will consider the qualities of the Self that reside in the Dwelling Place of Being.

Helpful Practices in the Dwelling Place of Tending

Tending Practice

If Tending is your weak quadrant on the Wheel of Change, you may want to deliberately strengthen your capacity to commit to something that requires long-term attention. I suggest an activity that will bring you pleasure over the long run. You could learn to tango, learn a new language, or learn to play a musical instrument that pleases your ear. Perhaps corresponding with a pen pal over many years or volunteering to help a child in your community learn to read would strengthen your tending muscles. Suspend your need for instant results and accept inadequacy along the way. Don't forget that you are committing to learn to abide the ups and downs of tending while finding satisfaction in the process of exercising your tending muscles.

Seek Out an Elder

Scan your relationship world to see if there is an older woman who is at ease with her aging, who looks back on her life with gratitude for all its twists and turns, who has sorted out what matters most to her in the end. Is there anything she might offer you? Is there anything you might offer her? Can you see who she is beneath the limitations of her aging? These precious relationships are always mutually enriching. In our modern society, elders are often introduced to this function by younger people who recognize their value and wisdom. As you nurture this special kind of friendship over time, you will likely learn something about tending the important things in life, and a great blessing will be bestowed on you.

Relaxing Ritual

If you are in a tending cycle that is taxing on your capacities, activities that emphasize a relaxed, sustained rhythm will be particularly nourishing to your body and your spirit. This could be a yoga or t'ai chi practice that includes particular awareness of breathing and of your heartbeat. A daily stretching routine, followed by stillness and an intentional focus on subtle sensations, can be relieving for your body temple and an over-exercised mind. Swimming or getting in a hot tub are soothing. Walking my dog, rain or shine, in the quiet of nearby hills is a staple for me. Light reading before going to sleep may draw your mind away from the demands of the day and condition your body for sleep.

Having FUN!

Those who are in sustained cycles of tending that require constant energy, attention, and care need to have some *fun* along the way. How about finding time to get good at a sport that you enjoy, or compiling a list of books that are entertaining and gripping and that carry you into another world. Intentional respites in locations that soothe your soul are good medicine and always well-deserved times of renewal. They may involve time alone, or frivolity with close friends. Bodywork, such as massage or acupuncture, keeps your vitality flowing. Baths are wonderful, with the door shut to the rest of household, complete with candles and music. Perhaps you love stargazing. Any activity that inspires awe and wonder is profoundly renewing. Your pleasure and physical comfort are not "extras" but essential ingredients of a balanced and happy life—especially during the inevitable challenges of a long tending cycle.

Adequate Rest

Rest is deeply restorative and crucial in alleviating the stress that comes with sustained vigilance and intensity. Daily napping for adults, even for as little as twenty minutes, is known to regenerate brain function and elevate mood. Reviving the siesta is not a bad idea. The injunction to get eight hours of sleep per night is not an overstatement. It has been proven that adequate sleep curbs inflammation, increases creativity, supports better memory, helps stabilize the heart, makes learning easier, improves sexual responsiveness, quickens your reaction time while driving, and elevates your mood. If you're having trouble sleeping, a consultation with a specialist may be warranted. Eastern medicine offers much in this field, including viable alternatives to addictive medications. Assessing your lifestyle habits—caffeine intake, night-owl tendencies, lack of exercise—will likely prove useful and lead to adjustments in your rest rhythms. Those who carry heavy tending responsibilities over time will benefit significantly from the healing function of the subconscious that naturally occurs in deep rest.

Eating Well and Exercising

Your body requires healthy sustenance for the long run. While corrective diets, supplements, and cleanses have their places, your primary sustenance for a long arc of tending will be healthy eating habits and regular exercise. Listen to what your body wants on both accounts, and establish a lifestyle that respects what you hear. Vitality and lightness of spirit are the antidotes to carrying weighty responsibility for long cycles. If you give your body the nutrients it needs and grant yourself rigorous daily movement, your frame of mind and your health will buoy you through commitments that may otherwise be wearing.

Resources

Joanna Macy and Molly Brown. *Coming Back to Life: The Updated Guide to the Work That Reconnects.* Gabriola Island, BC, Canada: New Society Publishers, 2014.

I include Joanna Macy's work for those whose calling relates to tending this earth. She is a true elder of this era who addresses the anguish experienced by those who would confront the harsh economic, social, and environmental realities of our time. She shows how grief, anger, and fear are healthy responses to threats to life that, when honored, can free us from paralysis or panic. Joanna includes communities of color as well as youth in *The Work That Reconnects*, and speaks directly to the positive potential of the corporate world. Her work profoundly affects people's outlooks and their ability to act in the world in sustainable and joyous ways.

Margaret J. Wheatley. *Perseverance*. Oakland, CA: Berrett-Koehler, 2010.

You might be wise to keep this small book of short passages beside your night table as you tend long-term commitments that matter deeply to you. Wheatley takes a bold look at the ties that bind us and at what impedes us—guilt, anger, fear, blame, boredom, loneliness—as well as at what supports our journey: steadfastness, choosing, clear seeing, play. She understands how these feelings, and our reticence to ask for what we really need, affect the directions our lives take. She urges us not to give in or give up; to examine our lives, thoughts, and experiences; and to "speak up about the things we care about." Wheatley encourages us to "rename ourselves," to "find a name that calls us to become fearless" and helps us develop our innate capacity for greatness, and that "calls us to our future self."

"Perhaps holding true to the vision and not losing our way is enough for one lifetime," Wheatley writes. This she has done. I cherish books like this, whose content is congruent with the author's lived experience.

open

spacious

embodied

at peace

one with all of life

whole

rhythmic

trusting

at home in myself

grateful

free

present

loving

authentic

compassionate

6

The Dwelling Place of Being: The Origin of Your Path

Enough talk for the night.
[S]He is laboring in me;

I need to be silent
for a while,

worlds are forming
in my heart.

MEISTER ECKHART

The Dwelling Place of Being, represented as the center of the Wheel of Change, is home. This central aspect of Self does not phase in or out with our cyclical experiences of change; Being is the dwelling place that holds them all. It is the origin of our life path. It is, as the Christian mystic Meister Eckhart wrote, "where worlds form." When we are still in the Dwelling Place of Being, we are particularly sensitive to what the Field of Possibility is holding for us.

Being is the quality of *presence* that we can feel in someone when she is at home in her own skin, at ease with things as they are, without feeling she has to project the "needs" or desires of her personality or ego. It is the domain of our deepest identity that abides beneath the roles we play, beneath the spectrum of feelings that we experience, and beneath the storyline of our lives. Being is ultimately one with the eternal wellspring of life that animates our universe and all that lives within it. I think of it as the realm of love. I believe that, even when the apparent ultimate ending occurs—when we shed our bodies—this essence of Being continues on in some way.

The quality of Being is ever-present, and we recognize it in the peace and comfort we find when we rest in our center. In our daily lives, we tend to move in and out of this dwelling place—but when heart and mind settle here, all the movement and challenge we experience is seen in a larger context. The stillness of Being quiets the heart, inspires fresh thinking, and awakens our sense of connection with trees and animals, neighbors and people who live on the other side of the globe—actually, with all of existence. Simplicity and clarity arise in the clear and uncluttered space of Being. From this Dwelling Place it is easiest to discern how to move effectively and heartfully into the world. What we then *do* carries transformational power and the qualities of lucidity, integration, and blessing.

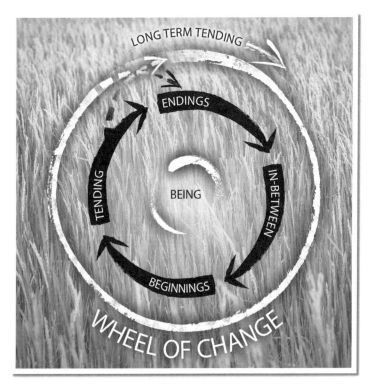

The Transformative Power of Being

Some enter the Dwelling Place of Being during quiet walks in nature. For others, the portal to this sanctuary opens within a practice of yoga or mindfulness. A cup of tea on the front porch may be another's key to the gate. The flow of gratitude opens the heart to this reality. Poet Mary Oliver calls prayer a doorway". . . into thanks, and a silence in which another voice may speak." Rumi opens the gateway to Being when he says, "There are hundreds of ways to kneel and kiss the ground."

Walking through your chosen doorway takes you beyond normal busyness and problem-solving into silence. Anne Dosher, a CIYO elder and friend, takes time every night before going to sleep to "put the day to bed." This ritual is an eleventh-century Anglican practice that was taught to her by her vicar when she was five years old. For three years, her grandmother sat beside her at bedtime, helping her with the practice. Even now, in her nineties, when Anne lays her head on her pillow at night, she scans the day, beginning with the most recent events and working back toward waking. With each vignette that comes to mind, she says, "Thank you," then ponders her handling of each circumstance, seeing what there is to learn from these encounters. Then she lets the day go and relaxes into the Dwelling Place of Being. Because her subconscious is clear and open when she goes to sleep, she often has dreams that bring guiding wisdom and insight to her waking life.

Anne also starts her day centered in the Dwelling Place of Being. The very first thing in the morning, she walks barefoot into her backyard, stands quietly in a central spot, and slowly turns in a full circle, blessing the waves of the day as they roll in. This practice has its roots in the tradition of the Native American pipe carrier, into which Anne has been initiated. She carefully brings to mind the people she knows who are in need, and anchors her day in the Dwelling Place of Being.

When Anne was in her eighties, after many decades of experience with large-scale systems change, the chief administrative officer of San Diego County asked her to join an advisory group charged with sorting out what the local press called "the County in chaos." Sensing Anne's value, his team members began quietly asking her to sit in on particularly difficult meetings, simply to be present and speak when she felt it might be helpful. She became known as the Elder Consultant, appreciated for both her deep knowledge of systems and the spirit in which she walked into the room. The CAO referred to Anne's steady "blessing presence." She describes the quality of those conversations as pivotal in "a County coming into its own," affecting the lives of millions.

The gifts we offer are amplified when the transformative power of Being carries them into the world.

Improvising as a Way of Life

The Dwelling Place of Being is not just peaceful self-contentment. It is the locus of an essential aliveness and wholeness that, unobstructed, unfurls into the dance of our living from one moment to the next.

Maryliz talks about the unique way she found this wellspring of inspiration in herself. In her early years she learned to play the pipe organ, and by age nine was accompanying well-known musicians in their performances. An exceptional organist as an adult, she was a magnet for her church's parishioners. With her choice of music and her delicate touch, Maryliz interpreted her minister's inspirational message, providing a soaring and heart-opening undercurrent for his words. She describes her inner process as "listening acutely to his script and amplifying the message through music written by well-known composers."

One day, following a service, her minister issued her a challenge: "You have mastered the score; perhaps it is time to move on to improvisation." Maryliz was willing to try, but leaving behind the mindset of accompanist to find the source out of which her own music could arise set her adrift. She lost her way and confidence, realizing that "Up to this point, I was very good at what I did, but *I* was missing." Letting music arise spontaneously to clothe the spirit of the moment would require accessing her own depths in a way she had never done before.

In the midst of this crisis, Maryliz was invited to join a team of women who work with terminally ill cancer patients in a residential retreat program. They wanted her to improvise music that would ease the suffering of the participants and help them find a place of peace in themselves. Maryliz started by listening deeply to the men and women sitting around her, and then, using percussion, keyboard, wind instruments, and her own voice, sounding out loud the impulses that arose in her:

> In the beginning, I could only bear two seconds of improvisation before retreating to known passages, for fear of getting lost. Finding my own line of music in the moment was a matter of deliberately slowing

down into a spacious interior rhythm. In my work as an accompanist I had tracked musical response to the world with my mind—and now my primary receptor had to be my heart.

Maryliz's willingness to surrender to this process has opened her ability to perceive a particular essence in a person that she perceives as sound. Using her instruments, she reflects that signature to those who have, in the intensity of their illness, lost connection with their intrinsic wholeness. In other words, she is guiding them into the Dwelling Place of Being.

One cancer patient she worked with was experiencing intense agitation as he neared the end of his life. Sitting with him, Maryliz intuitively began to use her voice and breath to magnify the core quality of Being that was layered over by his illness. Sensing that the specific note D-flat was his dominant home vibration, she proceeded to bathe him in this tone. She witnessed him gradually regain a tangible sense of "This is who I am." His anxiety calmed, and he began to reconcile himself with his life. Maryliz believes that his resonance with the D-flat tone gave him the confidence to face both his life as he had lived and his imminent death. A week later, he died peacefully.

Resting in her own Being, Maryliz can perceive not only the fundamental essence of an individual, but also the archetypal essence that lives in a shared collective consciousness. An experience of this at Grace Cathedral Church in San Francisco still reverberates in my bones. Matthew Fox and Brian Swimme had asked Maryliz to join them in a program honoring what they called the deep feminine. After speaking about the universal creative force that births and sustains all of life, they turned to Maryliz to "speak" about this energy through her medium of music, played on the majestic pipe organ in that cathedral. After sitting quietly for a long minute, Maryliz carefully placed her hands on the keys and her feet on the pedals. The magnificent sounds that emerged engulfed the cathedral in an awesome power and a tender sensitivity. At the conclusion of her piece, the congregation sat very still, tears flowing, filled with the glory of the feminine spirit.

Within the centered place of Being, our own unscripted voices await expression in ways unique to each of us. The capacity to access this center is the mark of an authentic life, one that is sourced from within. From that Dwelling Place of Being we endlessly unfold ourselves—through words, actions, decisions, and a myriad of artistic forms.

Being Informs All Phases of Transition

The Dwelling place of Being is at the center of the Wheel of Change because it is "the still point of the turning world," to borrow poet T.S. Eliot's phrase. As such, it informs and sustains all passing cycles of transition. But Being's presence in fact remains constant. Periodically returning to this inner home can anchor well-being when nothing else is clear. Friends or counselors who themselves know the Dwelling Place of Being are invaluable—their centering invites us into our own core identity.

What is the relationship between the Dwelling place of Being and each of the four phases of transition? And why is it placed at the center of the Wheel of Change?

In the discomfort and turmoil of the Dwelling Place of Endings, we can relax our grip on what is passing away and stabilize our experience in the peace of Being. A strengthened relationship with this immutable center can be the benediction of a rugged phase of ending.

The Dwelling Place of In-Between contains its own set of anxieties due to its unnerving requirement to live in the unknown. A disciplined return to one's quiet center reminds our minds and nervous systems that the deepest truth of Self does not undergo transition.

The Dwelling Place of New Beginnings heralds a dynamism that sweeps us forth from dormancy into forward movement. The frantic pace of the world can easily grab us at this point, disconnecting us from deeper levels of knowing. The challenge is to balance the call to action with continued reference to the still point of Being. When the oscillation between Being and Doing is in balance, the outer dynamics of our lives reflect the inner truth of who we really are and what we know to be true.

In the Dwelling Place of Tending we are called to steward responsibilities and commitments that matter to us. These undertakings do not *define* who we are. They are *evidence* of who we are. Beneath the activities of tending lies the quality of Being that informs these pursuits; we can count on its sustaining energy to help us bring our long-term commitments to fruition. The congruity between our abiding identity in spirit and our externalized expression is deeply fulfilling.

The entire Wheel of Change is oiled and balanced by the quality of presence at its hub: the Dwelling Place of Being. As you return to this center over and over, every stage of your transitions will be informed by the Field of Possibility, which holds your future and enables its unfolding in the most graceful way possible. This continual blossoming is at the heart of the Coming Into Your Own process. As we emerge together, this world is blessed and transformed by the healing and creative presence of the feminine.

Helpful Practices in the Dwelling Place of Being

An Invitation

In 2009, the CIYO faculty initiated a monthly Day of Silence for ourselves and graduates of the program. Seeking to support one another in our determination to live from the inside out, we realized that one of the best ways to do that would be to honor the common source from which all our paths originate: the Dwelling Place of Being. I now invite all of you who have walked this path of transition to join our global community of chosen silence.

The beauty of this virtual gathering is its inclusiveness—a flexibility that accommodates the daily rhythm of each participant. Women around the globe choose to spend all or some part of the last Sunday of each month in silence, as a regular touchstone into Being. There is no philosophical overlay, only a commitment to take some part of that day to switch off all technology and move at a slower pace that connects them to one another, to the earth, and most importantly to the Dwelling Place of Being within. A sacred web of connection binds us together, strengthens our resolve and, I believe, opens the door to our common origin as we rest together in this universal home. We can feel our collective return to Being rippling through countries and time zones, amplifying a homing signal that, amid the tumult of the world, resonates in every heart. If you would like to participate, send an e-mail request to pchick4@myfairpoint.net. My colleague Peri Chickering and I will include you in the inspirational reminder we send out each month.

Sitting Meditation

In earlier chapters I have suggested various forms of meditation. I want to reinforce these options again—they can connect you with the Dwelling Place of Being and the design for your life contained in the Field of Possibility. Sitting meditation is a particular form of meditation that involves finding a relaxed but upright seated posture that you can sit in for twenty minutes. Dropping into the state of consciousness available through this practice requires deliberately setting aside time to release daily concerns and attachment to figuring everything out. Sitting meditation helps you to breathe out the intensities of the day and step outside the incessant commentary of your thoughts. It is a time apart that involves no effort, only the release of passing thoughts, one by one. You may become aware of an atmosphere in and around you that feels soft, enlivening, and sacred; over time, you may become aware of a subtle flow of wholeness through your body. The fruits of this state can include tolerance for what is actually happening in your life, no matter how challenging it may be. You may arrive at a depth of contentment and gratitude for whatever your life contains. You may also experience a heightened perception of elegant and compassionate responses you can make to the needs of your circumstances.

Your meditation practice is a journey of discovery in and of itself, and it will likely shift forms over time to suit your inner need. To start, I suggest spending five minutes sitting quietly alone each day: no reading, no journaling, no technology.

Chanting Your Way into Being

When we chant, we place our attention on words, tones, or phrases that have been repeated for hundreds of years in different traditions to access the Dwelling Place of Being. When we rest in the repetition of the chant for a few precious minutes, or perhaps a delicious half hour, the soul gets a needed break from the steady yammering of the mind. At the same time, the sanctified phrases gradually chip away at layers of doubt, resistance, fear, or worry that wall off the small, limited self from the expansive Being that each of us is becoming. Ananda Foley, a graduate of the CIYO program, offers a simple practice that could be helpful the next time you're buzzing with anxiety or heavy with sadness:

> Create the sound "So" and hold it for several seconds. Then form the sound "Hum," also for several seconds. Breathe as needed. After five to seven rounds of this, be still and notice the effects in your body. That silky-smooth quality of space behind your eyes or around your head is yours to keep.

Body-Centered Meditation

Here again we mention body-centered practices such as yoga, t'ai chi, and qigong, that were developed centuries ago as gateways to Being. Each accentuates the body's miraculous energetic circuitry, which is designed to unite personal experience with the universal flow. Find a teacher whom you like, or buy an instructional video, and open the spacious world that lives within you, between your very cells.

Bathe Your Soul in Art

Poets who themselves reside in the Dwelling Place of Being have the gift of inviting you to join them there. Their words can gently guide you into your own center. You may want to read the poetry of Rumi, Kabir, Mary Oliver, David Whyte, or Rilke. Find the poets who speak to your soul, and savor your relationship with them. Reading the poems aloud often helps you find the place of origin in you from which the poet wrote.

Visual art and music are other languages of the heart, when spoken by artists and musicians who create from "the still point of the turning world." Fill your life with their inspiration, and walk through the gateways they open into the Dwelling Place of Being.

. . . and simply . . .

Return home by laying one hand over your heart and the other over your solar plexus. Then, slowly breathe into both of your palms at once, and breathe out through your nose. The dominance of your thoughts will recede, your heart will open, and the Dwelling Place of Being will gently unfurl inside you.

Resources

Adyashanti. *The Way of Liberation: A Practical Guide to Spiritual Enlightenment.* San Jose, CA: Open Gate Sangha, 2013. Free download at www.adyashanti.org/library/The_Way_of_Liberation_Ebook.pdf.

I include this book for those who are seriously interested in opening a deeper sense of Self. Contained in the short, direct text is one of the best descriptions of Being that I have come across. Adyashanti's meditation instruction is simple and profound. In his preface he writes of his intention to help readers awaken from their imagined status as a person to who they really are. I enjoy this honest warning: "Applying these teachings may be damaging to your beliefs, disorienting to your mind, and distressing to your ego. From the perspective of waking up to reality these are good things to be cultivated."

Cynthia Bourgeault. *Centering Prayer and Inner Awakening.* Cambridge, MA: Cowley Publications, 2004.

This is a complete guidebook for those who wish to experience Centering Prayer. Bourgeault examines how the practice is related to the classic tradition of Christian contemplation, looks at the distinct nuances of its method, and explores its revolutionary potential to transform Christian life.

Anne LeClaire. *Listening Below the Noise*. New York, NY: HarperCollins Publications, 2009.

When Anne LeClaire decided to turn an ordinary Monday into a day of silence, she viewed her experiment as a one-time occurrence. Little did she realize she had begun an inner voyage that would transform her life. In the seventeen years since, LeClaire has practiced total silence on the first and third Monday of each month. By detaching herself from the bustle of her hectic lifestyle and learning to listen to her deepest self, she has found a center from which to live—one that tests, strengthens, and heals her. In practicing silence, she has discovered her own secret garden—a cloistered, sacred, private place where true personal growth is possible.

Mark Nepo. *The Book of Awakening: Having the Life You Want by Being Present to the Life You Have*. San Francisco, CA: Conari Press, 2000.

Every page of this book brings me home to myself. Through touching stories told in everyday language, Mark Nepo gently opens a new experience of freedom while living in the roughness and pleasures of life. This daybook is a summons to reclaim aliveness, liberate the Self, take life one day at a time, and savor the beauty offered by life's unfolding—regardless of your storyline. *The Book of Awakening* is the result of Nepo's own personal journey of the soul. Reading a passage each day will uncover the solid ground in yourself from which your path unfolds. I cherish the mature joy his writing awakens in me. This book is like a drink of fresh spring water every morning.

Epilogue

Celebrating Being

As my mother nears the end of her life, her greatest pleasure, despite bad eyesight and poor hearing, is to sit on the bench outside her front door with her wild bird friends. Just *being*. While my mother has been my greatest champion in supporting women coming into their own, her greatest gift to me has been her innate ability to speak to the apple tree, Being to Being. It is this quality of Self that my sister and I talk about when we consider what we will honor in her memorial service, when that time comes.

We are not interested in displaying all of her achievements: how she broke many a glass ceiling; her work to legitimize the study of science for girls in the United States; her leadership in education. These images of our mother in her professional roles crowd our early memories. But what is most meaningful for us is her sensitive connection with the natural world, where she was utterly herself—where her quality of Being shows through.

Our most intimate times with our mother were simple—as she separated irises in the garden, or played with her golden retriever, Tena. We have warm memories of vacationing in Montana, where we religiously walked at dawn and at dusk to the river that ran in front of our cabin, fly-fishing gear in hand, ever hopeful of catching dinner. It was my mother, however, who always called the brown trout out of hiding, while the rest of us came back empty-handed. I remember songbirds coming to sit on her head and shoulders in her later years. Through her relationships with plants and animals, she most fully reflected the oneness of all things and legitimized my own connectedness to all living beings.

To write the ending of this book, I felt I needed a particular atmosphere to draw me into the Dwelling Place of Being—the place from which all of these words sprang, and the place I will return to after the book is completed. I traveled to the Jedediah Smith Redwoods State Park, in northern California, near our home in southern Oregon. An especially magnificent campsite opened up quite unexpectedly, and I settled into the stillness of the old-growth redwoods. Early the next morning, my dog, Koa, and I crossed a walking bridge that spanned a crystal-clear river to deliver us into a protected grove of ancient trees. These "standing people," as the Tolowa people refer to them, have stood in place there for as long as 2,000 years. I called to Koa in a whisper, keeping her close out of respect for the presence of these towering elders. As my internal chatter receded, my eyes welled up with tears. Engulfed in what felt like an eternal silence, I felt myself intimately connected to the Great Mother.

Walking on the soft path under the dark canopy, I found myself thinking about why this patch of ground has been set aside as a State Park, noting the clear-cuts that press into the boundaries of the park. Certainly, it is to preserve the last four percent of the old-growth red-woods on the West Coast of the United States from the encroachments of human greed and insensitivity. But, I thought, something more draws people from all over the world to slowly walk these paths. Here they can remember and inhabit a wild and sacred part of the earth—and of themselves—that is in danger of extinction in the wake of civilization's progress.

My pondering was interrupted by the appearance of a slight East Indian woman walking toward us on the path. Koa greeted her eagerly, and I asked her why she was here in this grove at so early an hour. She said it reminded her of Bodhgaya, in India. It was there, she explained, under the sacred Bodhi Tree, that the Buddha experienced his awakening. Today, pilgrims travel from afar to walk on the path that encircles a descendant of that original tree. The young woman told me that she had come to this grove to ease the sorrow of a devastating childhood that was filled with the same kind of abuse that her sisters, mother, cousins, aunts, and grandmother experienced. She felt the deep silence and mighty presence of these trees as a strong healing force that could put an end to this succession. As we said goodbye, I could sense the deep peace she had found there.

I continued on my way in the presence of those stately trees that so simply and profoundly embodied the spirit of Being. The perimeter path around these sentinels reminded me of the ever-turning cycles of Endings, In-Between phases, New Beginnings, and sustained cycles of Tending that we all experience. In that stand of redwoods I felt the interconnection of all things and the gifts of our endings and beginnings, all held in the Field of Possibility. As this truth broke open into wonder, I felt how our personal cycles of transition align with great cycles of decline and renewal. I was ready to finish the long tending of a work of love, and knew I could trust the unfolding of the next steps in my life journey.

Afterword
by Margaret Wheatley

The wisdom offered in *Coming Into Your Own* provides a clear path for us women to transform ourselves personally. I would like to enlarge our vision and emphasize that our own desires to grow and change have an even greater purpose, far beyond our individual lives. We are alive and awake at a time when the planet—Gaia—is summoning us to develop our voice, our confidence, and our wise actions on behalf of life. I have gradually opened to this larger perspective, to the realization that I am working with and for life, and that life reciprocates in supporting me in mysterious but reliable ways. And in the process, my life has become delightful, magical, and filled with energy that contradicts my physical age!

Here are a few of my learnings that I offer in support of you trusting this larger view:

Life can only create growth and newness through a passage in the dark realms of lost meaning, lost relationships, lost confidence in our present identity. When I've been in the midst of this darkness, knowing that this is life's unavoidable cycle has been a lifeline. It isn't that I have failed or been victimized, but rather that life is preparing me to be stronger and more confident for the work ahead (btw it still feels like hell in the middle of it).

Gaia is speaking through us women as clearly as we are willing to trust and give voice to what we know. She is calling us to offer our wisdom and compassion for a world that has lost its way, that has forgotten how interconnected we are, that denies the necessity of relationships. Too many have forgotten or deny that we are innately caring, generous, and creative, that humans get through the hardest of times by staying together. As we women remember who we can be as fully human beings, we have Gaia's support for us in her many manifestations of animals, plants, and energies. We simply have to trust in this support.

We stand on the strong shoulders of our women ancestors. They persevered and so can we. As one spiritual teacher said: "It's just our turn to serve the world." I find great comfort in this and often wonder if things seem harder to us now because we've had it so easy for so long. We can get past our hesitation and fears by invoking our ancestors whose perseverance made our lives possible. It's our turn, and it's no big deal.

Margaret Wheatley, author of eight books, the most recent one being *How Does Raven Know? Entering Sacred World–A Meditative Memoir.* This intimate reflection was written after her 70th birthday and published in 2014. It is available at www. margaretwheatley.com. She describes this personal account:

"*How Does Raven Know?* invites you to see the world anew informed not by science but by sacred wisdoms. I have sought to encourage you to shift your gaze to discover the support, confidence, and companionship we need to meet this time. My aspiration is to reintroduce you to a world we modern ones have dismissed or ignored, a world still held for us in the ancient wisdom traditions of most cultures. It is not a call to action, but to relationship with forgotten companions and animate Earth that, in my own experience, willingly offer us support, encouragement, and consolation."

Acknowledgments

My deepest gratitude to the women who offered their own experiences in candid stories as touchstones for others. I couldn't use all of the stories, but the substance of each has been carefully woven into this book.

The work of the CIYO programs is being carried further in the world by a band of courageous, generous, gorgeous, bad-ass pioneers: the facilitators of our CIYO programs. I honor and thank you all from the depths of my heart. Много благодаря, Duizendmaal dank, Merci beaucoup, Danke schön, Molte grazie, Muchas gracias, Teşekkür ederim, أشكرك كثيراً, ありりがとうござ います, thank you very much.

Shoshana Alexander, a bow to you for extraordinary editing, propelling me into excellence, and teaching me to write while you were at it. Richard Lehnart, besides being a topnotch copy editor, you were a keel on my boat in the last stages of completion of the book. Cornelius Matteo, you are an excellent photographer and a friend. Christy Collins, I trust your aesthetic as a designer. Thank you, Steve Scholl, for seeing the value of this work and supporting it through White Cloud Press.

Huge appreciation to a host of friends who traveled with me through the cycles of tending this work of love, and who forgave me for being less than available at times, including: Ellen Faith, Maggie Alexander, Sahni Hamilton, Michele Steckler, Peri Chickering, Cindy Saunders, Sarah-Jane Menato, Suzanne Anderson, Carol

Ingram, Greg Jemsek, Kelvy Bird, Jennifer Zeitler, Jane Hunter, Anna Celestino, and many other dear friends.

The generous artists and poets who donated their work understand the spirit of this book and are themselves beacons of light.

Tender gratitude to my mother, who believes in me without reserve. Anita, you're the best sister ever. And Michael, I could never have finished this without your loving support and steadfast partnership.

Appendices

A Guide for Reading Groups and Women's Circles

Coming Into Your Own: A Woman's Guide Through Life Transitions lends itself beautifully to groups of women who are interested in exploring the nature of change and in getting some traction in their own evolving lives. It would be important for participants to agree together whether this will be a discussion group and/or an actual sharing of personal experience based on a common reading of the book. What I suggest here, as a format and process, is a combination of the two—I feel it would be hard to read the book while keeping your own life experience at arm's length.

Whether you form a group for these purposes or choose this book as the centerpiece of an ongoing discussion group, it will be important to establish parameters for the duration of the life of the group. I suggest that you:

- Determine the number of times you will meet. Six sessions of 90 minutes to two hours each would work nicely. I'd do it in a private setting, and not over a meal, so that each speaker will have the full attention of the group.

- Designate a facilitator for each session who can make sure that each woman gets to speak and that any parameters that have been unanimously agreed on are observed. This person could find a poem to open the session with, and end it on a note of appreciation. When there is a Round, in which each woman speaks in turn, the facilitator should keep track of the time to ensure that each woman gets a chance to express herself.

• Make two agreements as a group that will enhance openness in your circle. First, I suggest making an explicit agreement of confidentiality. This means the freedom to share your impressions of the book and your personal experience with others outside the group, but *not* to speak of the experiences of others in the group. The second agreement is *not* to drift into attempts to fix one another. These are not problem-solving sessions, but times for reflection. Insights will come to each along the way, but not from advice from others in the circle. If one group member begins to counsel another, anyone in the circle (the designated facilitator in particular) should note the drift in this direction and kindly ask for a return to simple support and appreciation.

Week 1
(presuming all have read Chapter 1)

Opening Dialogue

A look at the Wheel of Change is a useful starting place. Begin with a discussion of the map to ensure that everyone understands it.

Round

Go around the circle, allowing each person to speak without interruption to express where she now sees herself on the Wheel of Change and why she would locate herself in that particular Dwelling Place.

It might be interesting to draw the Wheel of Change on a piece of posterboard and mark where each group member sees herself, so that you have a profile of your entire group.

Discuss

Have you ever felt the Field of Possibility at work in your life?

Do you feel that some inherent potential lives in you that wants fuller expression?

Make sure that each woman has a chance to speak and that she feels listened to.

Week 2
(having read Chapter 2)

Opening Dialogue

What does it mean to do an ending "well"?

What does it look like to avoid an ending, or to rush through it without proper acknowledgment?

What do endings feel like?

Round

Each woman speaks about a current or past ending that is vivid in her awareness.

In reading chapter 2, what has she learned about endings that may be relevant to this current situation, or may provide insight about how she engaged a significant ending in the past?

Week 3
(having read Chapter 3)

Opening Dialogue

In your own words, describe the Dwelling Place of In-Between.

How do you know if you are in it?

How do you hold this Dwelling Place open when the world doesn't understand the need for an interim space?

Round

Each woman recalls a current or past experience of the Dwelling Place of In-Between and shares what it was/is like to be in a void between an ending and a new beginning.

Were you aware of deliberately protecting a period of time to heal, slow down, and reflect?

What are the conditions in which you can best wait for inner guidance and listen for impulses from the Field of Possibility?

Week 4
(having read Chapter 4)

Opening Dialogue

What struck you in a new way in the chapter on the Dwelling Place of New Beginnings?

Did you have any fresh insights about how to approach the initiation of a new cycle or endeavor in your life?

Round

Is there a chapter of your life that is opening now?

If your life were a book, what would be the title of this chapter?

Is this title related to a deeper thread of purpose that you are becoming aware of in your life?

How can you test the new direction on a small scale to make sure you are on track?

Week 5
(having read Chapter 5)

Opening Dialogue

What resonates with you in the chapter on Tending?

Is there anything in this consideration that sparks new thoughts or insights?

Round

What are you tending right now that requires a long-term commitment?

What is it like to dedicate yourself to its fulfillment over time?

What kind of support do you need to fulfill this commitment?

Week 6
(having read Chapter 6 and the Epilogue)

Because *being* is hard to talk about, I suggest an activity that is more intuitive. Prepare for this final session by bringing old magazines to cut up, a piece of white poster-board for each person, scissors, crayons, and glue sticks. In the first half hour of your session, make collages that represent your experience (or lack of experience) in the Dwelling Place of Being. It is best to do this in silence or with soft, unobtrusive music in the background.

Round

Each woman presents what she has assembled. Comments are welcome that reflect appreciation for who this woman is in her essence.

Think of a celebratory way to close this sixth and final session.

Further Resources for Women in Transition

I maintain a list of high-quality programs that may be of assistance to you at particular moments in your process of transition and transformation. You can find this list at www.endingsandbeginnings.com, the companion website to *Coming Into Your Own: A Woman's Guide Through Life Transitions.* Also available on the site are references to specific people who have refined particular offerings to augment your passage into a new phase of your life.

You will also find there a list of women trained in leading the Symbols Way Process, and who may be able to help you get unstuck so that you may walk more easily your path into the future.

About the Coming Into Your Own Program

The deep roots of the CIYO program were planted in a women's circle whose founders were three of the seven members of the Circle of Seven: Anne Dosher, MaryBeth Christie (now Redmond), Serena Newby, Leslie Lanes, Glennifer Gillespie, Beth Jandernoa, and me, Barbara Cecil. The Circle had originally gathered in 1995 to develop an initiation program for women, but we soon realized that we were the ones who needed a rite of passage through our own health crises, divorces, family and job challenges, etc. After four years of regular retreats in which we experimented on ourselves, we were asked to create a program for young women who wanted to live on their terms rather than follow a formulaic approach to "fulfillment." Only at this point did we feel we had something to offer.

The deep principles that produce the magic and the sustained effects of the CIYO program were realized in the long-term commitment that we of the Circle of Seven made to one another, the improvised processes we created to coax out the emergent potential of each one and of the group, and the cherishing of our collective spirit, which we named the Circle Being (See: http://www.collective-wisdominitiative.org/papers/circleof7_interv.htm).

The Young Women's Mentorship Program was funded in 1995 with a research grant from the Fetzer Institute. Barbara Cecil, Glennifer Gillespie, and Beth Jandernoa facilitated the maiden voyage of this program, which eventually evolved into Coming Into Your Own. Word spread of participants' increased confidence, effectiveness, and clarity of purpose as a result of the supportive environment and carefully constructed reflective processes that comprised the CIYO course. By 2015, more than 4,000 women and a number of men had been inspired by their experience in some version of the program. It is now taught, by a cadre of skilled facilitators, in seven languages by faculty who reside in seventeen nations.

The CIYO course is designed to help women find their footing in the midst of life transitions and, ultimately, to discern their calling as it seeks expression now. CIYO courses help women shape a direction that is relevant in today's world. Wholeness and balance in ourselves are crucial if we are to truly address the fragmentation in the world and the barrenness of so many workplaces.

Course offerings can be found on the CIYO website: www.CIYOwomensretreat.com.

About the Symbols Way Process

A pivotal part of the CIYO course is participation in a reflective process called the Symbols Way. Most of the CIYO faculty are trained to facilitate this process and are in position to guide this experience, either in person or via Skype. A list of certified guides and their contact information can be found on the companion website for this book: www.endingsandbeginnings.com.

The Symbols Way helps women (and men) make choices that respect the deeper purpose of their lives. The process leads to personal clarity and practical next steps that are rooted in one's essential identity. It is a way of connecting with the potential for your life that is held in the Field of Possibility.

The thread of your calling shows up differently at different stages of your life, and sometimes disappears from view, hiding in dark recesses. The Symbols Way invites that deeper theme out of hiding. It offers a way to embrace your life in all its peculiarities, and points to practical next steps on your path into the future. It usually takes 90 minutes to two hours.

About the Artists

Page xiii, Suzanne Magat, *Apples,* oil on canvas, 1918. This was painted by my Russian grandmother, inspired by Van Gogh.

Page 1, Vincent Van Gogh, *Green Wheat Fields with Cypress*, oil on canvas, 1889.

Page 19, Barbara Cecil, *Georgia O'Keeffe's Courtyard*, oil on canvas, © 2009. Painted in my beloved Abiquiu, New Mexico.

Page 22, Leslie Lee, *Do or Do Not, There is No Try,* oil on canvas, © 2004. Leslie is a Portland, Oregon, artist who graciously donated use of her work. This is available as a print or as cards. Visit Meiners & Lee Studios www.meinersandlee.com.

Page 65, Carol Ingram, *Goodbye,* oil on canvas, © 2015. Carol is an Ashland, Oregon, artist who generously offered use of this painting. You may visit www.carolingramart.com to view her gallery, including the original of this piece.

Page 105, Meganne Forbes, *Hummingbird Spiral*, watercolor, © 2014. Meganne is a visionary artist who honors the earth and all its inhabitants by painting them. Please visit her website www.meganneforbes.com to see what she loves.

Page 137, Leon Lhermitte, *The Distaff Girl,* 1865. The distaff is a spindle onto which flax is wound as it is spun.

Page 145, Sylvia Pastore, *The Gardener,* © 2000. Sylvia's magical world of imagination gifts *Coming Into Your Own.* Her painting is about finding beauty in everyday life. She lives in the UK, where she paints and tends the natural world around her farm. www.silviapastore.com.

Page 167, Barbara Cecil, *Portrait of Anne Dosher, Elder,* © 2010.

Page 183, Emily Carr, *Forest,* 1931–33, oil on canvas, 118.2 x 76.1 cm, Collection of the Vancouver Art Gallery, Emily Carr Trust. Emily Carr is a Canadian artist who cherished the earth and its indigenous people. Her coming into her own story and her art have been great inspirations to me.

Cover Art

Carol Ingram and Barbara Cecil, *Emergence,* © 2015. I love that two women collaborated to paint a painting. Carol has been a great friend and inspiration to me.

Photography

I am thankful for Cornelius Matteo, who photographed many of the paintings: www.cmatteophotography.com.

About the Author

Barbara Cecil's Master's degree in Speech Communication and Human Relations has supported her in her calling to assist individuals, groups, teams, and organizations toward the full manifestation of their creative potential. For twenty years she worked in various parts of the world as a consultant specializing in large systems change, with an emphasis on organizational learning. For eight years she served as an Associate Dean of the School of Humanities at California State University, Long Beach.

In her travels in the former Soviet Union, South Africa, the Near East, Europe, and North America, Barbara witnessed the effects of women finding their voices and assuming their full stature. Believing that the serious challenges facing the world at this time need the perspective, sensitivities, and collaborative instincts of feminine leadership, she began to support women coming into their own. Since 1995, when she began mentoring young women leaders, Barbara has created refined settings in which women from all walks of life discover the unique expressions of their personal and work lives—and, most important, come into alignment with the beauty and uniqueness of their innermost beings.

Barbara and her husband live in Ashland, Oregon, where she spends happy hours in her painting studio and cares for their land as if the life of the planet depended on their stewardship of it.

Barbara is available for coaching, presentations, and program facilitation. She is also interested in training coaches and therapists in use of The Symbols Way, and can be reached through her website: www.endingsandbeginnings.com.